# Special-Occ

# Table Runners

## JANET CARIJA BRANDT

Bothell, Washington

## ACKNOWLEDGMENTS

First and foremost, a big thank-you to Melissa Lowe for suggesting this book and encouraging me to do it. It has been an enormous amount of fun. To my always-willing and ever-helpful elves—Debby Eads, Deb Haggard, Brian Haggard, Suzanne Borse, and Jan Paul—a big thank-you for your stunning contributions. Thank you to King's Road and National Nonwovens for beautiful fabrics to play with. Thank you to Sharon Rose for a careful and thoughtful edit and to the multitalented crew at Martingale and Company. In particular, thanks to Nancy Martin, Brent Kane, Cleo Nollette, and Cheryl Stevenson for their creative efforts in photographing all of the table runners. And most of all, I thank the one who makes my creative life possible: my husband, Chris.

## CREDITS

President . . . . . . . . . . . . . . . . . . . . . Nancy J. Martin

CEO/Publisher . . . . . . . . . . . . . . . . Daniel J. Martin

Associate Publisher . . . . . . . . . . . . Jane Hamada

Editorial Director . . . . . . . . . . . . . . Mary V. Green

Design and Production Manager . . . . Cheryl Stevenson

Text Designer . . . . . . . . . . . . . . . . . Stan Green

Cover Designer . . . . . . . . . . . . . . . . Cheryl Stevenson

Technical Editor . . . . . . . . . . . . . . . Sharon Rose

Copy Editor . . . . . . . . . . . . . . . . . . Liz McGehee

Proofreader . . . . . . . . . . . . . . . . . . Leslie Phillips

Illustrator . . . . . . . . . . . . . . . . . . . . Lisa McKenney

Photographer . . . . . . . . . . . . . . . . . Brent Kane

That Patchwork Place, Inc.,
is an imprint of Martingale & Company.

Special-Occasion Table Runners
© 1999 by Janet Carija Brandt

Martingale & Company, PO Box 118, Bothell, WA 98041-0118 USA

Printed in the United States of America
04 03 02 01 00 99        6 5 4 3 2 1

**Library of Congress Cataloging-in-Publication Data**

Brandt, Janet Carija,
   Special-occasion table runners / Janet Carija Brandt.
      p.   cm.
   ISBN 1-56477-239-X
   1. Patchwork—Patterns.   2. Quilting—Patterns.
   3. Appliqué—Patterns.   4. Runners (Household linens)   I. Title.
   TT835.B655   1999                                98–42876
   746.44'50436—dc21                                   CIP

## MISSION STATEMENT

We are dedicated to providing quality products and service by working together to inspire creativity and to enrich the lives we touch.

# CONTENTS

# INTRODUCTION

So many memories are made when we gather around the tables in our homes. Sharing the day's news at the kitchen table over after-school milk and cookies, listening to grandparents reminisce after a special dinner in the dining room, or playing board games on the coffee table in front of a roaring fire on a cold winter afternoon are just a few of the countless moments when family and friends are brought together.

Tables in most homes are called upon to serve in many ways. More than a place to share a meal or a cup of coffee, they are the nerve centers of families. You might plan a family vacation, make an important decision, enforce a curfew, or roll out Christmas cookies all in the same spot. And of course, the little tables in our homes play many roles, too. A bedside table might normally hold nothing more than a good reading lamp and a clock, but when you're sick, it becomes your whole universe. Tissues and medicines compete with hot tea, fresh flowers, lots of books, and, if you're my kid, a little bell to summon Mom to the bedside.

So what can we do to celebrate these little centers of family life? Let's drape them according to the season in colorful, stylish runners, creating a tabletop wardrobe!

# THE BASICS OF TABLE DRESSING

My parents were retailers when I was growing up, and I started doing display work at a very early age. I still enjoy displaying things in my home. Tabletops are a natural spot to arrange and rearrange linens, fabrics, dishes, and neat stuff. Lots of neat stuff. Few people understand why I like my monkey candlesticks, old milk glass, bits and pieces of layered fabric, red trivets, or Russian samovars. One entire tabletop in my studio is devoted to neat stuff. Seeing it out in the light of day gives me pleasure, inspires me, and reminds me of what I have!

Tabletops can be dressed up for special occasions or for everyday enjoyment. The basic elements are the same: the table, the covering, and the settings or accessories. A bare table can be covered with a cloth, runner, tray, doily, or set of coasters or place mats. Any of these can be used alone or layered. How to best employ and enjoy table runners is the focus of this book.

Table runners can be practical or pretty or both. They work well atop dining room tables, buffets, kitchen tables or islands, coffee or tea tables, hall or sofa tables, and nightstands. Use them to protect and decorate for everyday use, or to set the mood for a special occasion.

A table runner can be used alone or layered over one or two tablecloths. One of my favorite resources for tablecloths are the remnant piles at upholstery and drapery shops. I give the remnants a minimum of finishing, perhaps pinking the edges or fringing just the cut sides.

Here are some creative ways to use runners:

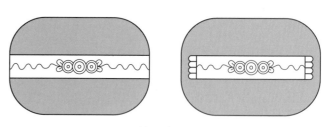

Use alone.

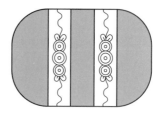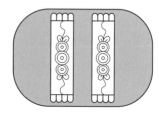

Use in pairs.

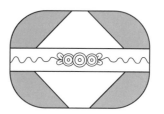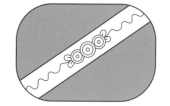

Use in conjunction with a tablecloth or remnant.　　　Use on an angle.

Table runners are an exciting way to add color to your decor, but how do you choose a color scheme? Some holidays have a built-in scheme. Red and green are always a sure bet for Christmas, but this is also a great color combo in a rustic country or folksy setting. The colors of the seasons themselves dictate other schemes, such as the pastels of spring or the golden reds and oranges of fall. The colors of the room or the colors of your favorite dishes and accessories can also suggest a color scheme.

# CUSTOMIZING DESIGNS TO FIT YOUR TABLE

Measure the table you want to dress. Mentally, or with a quick sketch, visualize how you want the runner to look on your table. Should it be long, short, wide, or narrow? Do you want it to hang over the edges? For an even better idea of how the runner will look, make a pattern out of newspaper, trimming until it's just the right size and shape for your table.

Longer

Wider

Next, you have to decide about the appliquéd or embroidered designs on the runner. Do you want them to flow over the table edge, or do you want them centered on the tabletop?

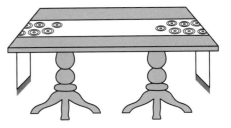

Design over edge

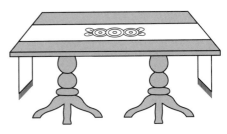

Design in center

The designs in this book can be customized to fit a table of any length or shape. As the term "runner" implies, most of these projects "run" the length of the table, but there is no reason they can't run diagonally or across the width of the table. You can also adapt the designs to fit a circular, oval, or square tabletop.

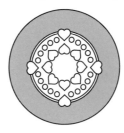

Circle

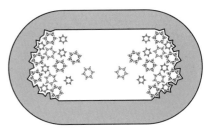

Oval

Square
Set a square on point with the corners hanging over.

**NOTE:** *Project directions are written for a certain-size runner. You will need to adjust the yardage requirements if you want to make a different size.*

Another way to customize your design is to choose a creative shape and/or edge treatment for the short ends of a rectangular runner. Below are some different shapes and edge treatments to choose from:

You'll find design options at the end of the instructions for each project.

**Shapes for Ends of Table Runners**

**Finishes for Ends of Table Runners**

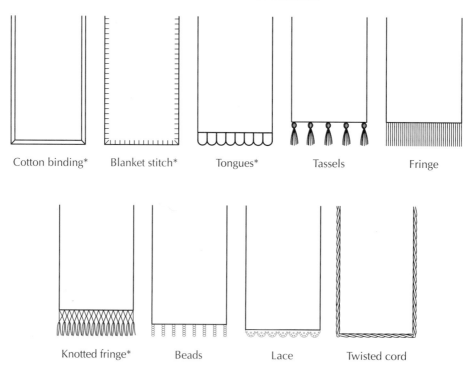

Cotton binding*     Blanket stitch*     Tongues*     Tassels     Fringe

Knotted fringe*     Beads     Lace     Twisted cord

*Instructions given

# TOOLS AND SUPPLIES

✓ Yardstick or measuring tape (for measuring your table)

✓ Rotary cutter, cutting mat, and straight-edge cutting guide

✓ #08 crewel needles

✓ Pins (for appliqué; 1" are my favorite)

✓ Embroidery floss

✓ Paper scissors

✓ Fabric scissors

✓ Sewing machine

✓ Thread

✓ Pigma pen

✓ Pencil

✓ Template material (see page 8)

✓ 18"-wide roll of tracing paper (for felt cutwork; available at craft and office-supply stores)

✓ Fusible web (for cotton appliqué)

# FABRICS

My appliqué technique is different from those you might be used to. Instead of turning the raw edge under and using a traditional appliqué stitch, I use a hand-sewn blanket stitch to finish the raw edge and secure the piece to the background in one step. This means I do not add seam allowances to my appliqué patterns. This technique is well suited to wool and felt, but can also be adapted for cotton. It is quick and easy (no more turning under those tight points and curves), and gives my work a folk-art look I really like.

Though simple, my appliqué method requires careful choice of fabric. In this book, you will find wool-on-wool runners, felt runners, and cotton runners, plus a few that combine two kinds of fabric. Most of the projects can be made with any fabric. For example, "My Valentine" (page 17) and "Easter Baskets" (page 32) are wool-on-wool

appliqué but could be done in cotton or felt. Likewise, "Snowflakes" (page 21) and "Happy Birthday, Little Bear!" (page 25) are done in cotton but would be fun and easy to translate into wool or felt. The only exception to this is felt cutwork; felt must be used for this technique.

## Wool

Use woven 100%-wool flannel for the best results. Wool now appears in many quilt shops as well as traditional fabric shops. Another source is used clothing, whether from your closet or the local secondhand store. Look for a tightly woven fabric with the weight and feel of a favorite wool skirt. Loosely woven wools, such as tweeds and bouclés, and lightweight varieties that drape well, such as challises, are harder to work with.

The rules for working with wool are simple. Begin by prewashing all wool, whether new or "recycled." Machine wash in warm water with regular laundry detergent on a regular cycle. Machine dry on normal or low setting. The wool will shrink slightly and come out of the dryer all fluffy. This is a felting technique called "fulling."

## Felt

Another option for your project is felt. The felt you usually see in fabric and craft stores is made from acrylic. I like to use a wool/rayon blend with 20% to 50% wool. (See "Resources" on page 58 for a great source.)

Wool felt has some big advantages over the acrylic variety. The biggest advantage is that wool edges stay crisp whether cut straight or with a decorative cutter. Decoratively cut edges do not have to be finished with a blanket stitch, greatly reducing the amount of handwork. Wool-blend felts can be hand dyed for unlimited color choices, another big advantage for quilters.

You can machine wash and dry wool felt for a different look. The surface becomes textured and the hand is very soft. Iron it and it returns to its usual smooth finish. Beware: Many commercially dyed wool-blend felts are not colorfast. They must be dry-cleaned. Check the care instructions when you buy them.

## Cotton

Tightly woven 100% cotton works best for appliqué. Preshrink by machine washing and drying, then pressing. Cotton is affordable and comes in an almost infinite array of colors and patterns. Choose cotton if you want to work with prints and/or if you want to incorporate any piecing into your runner design.

# TRANSFERRING PATTERNS

I use templates to transfer appliqué designs onto fabric. The choice of template material depends on the shape of the appliqué piece and how many pieces you need. Mark the right side of your template and always trace and cut on the right side of your fabric, or the design will be reversed. Skip this step if you plan to use the cotton mini-fuse technique described on the next page.

**Tracing Paper:** For simple shapes that will be used only once or twice, I recommend tracing-paper templates. Trace the pattern from the book onto tracing paper. Cut out. Pin the paper pattern to the right side of your fabric and cut around the pattern. Do not add seam allowances at any point.

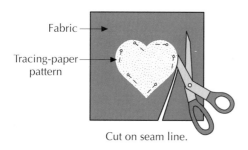

Fabric

Tracing-paper pattern

Cut on seam line.

**Template Plastic:** Use the lightweight template plastic sold in quilt shops to make templates for pieces you will use several times. Trace the pattern from the book onto the plastic sheet. Cut out. Lay the plastic template on the right side of your fabric and trace around it, using a chalk pencil or the marking tool of your choice. Hold the template very firmly, especially with wool, which has a

tendency to stretch and pull. Cut along the marked line. Do not add seam allowances at any point.

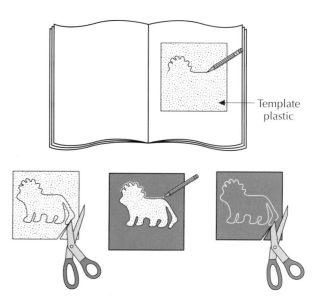

Template plastic

**Interfacing:** For pattern pieces that are highly detailed or that will be used many times, I recommend making templates of lightweight, nonfusible interfacing. Interfacing can be pinned and works well for fabrics that are difficult to mark, such as wool. Trace the pattern from the book directly onto the interfacing. Cut out. Pin the interfacing template to the right side of your fabric. Cut around the interfacing. Do not add seam allowances at any point.

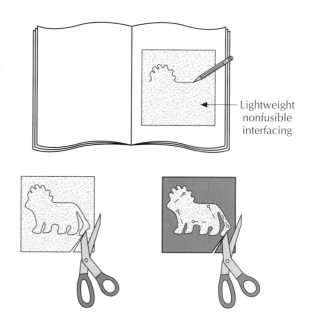

Lightweight nonfusible interfacing

# Appliqué Techniques

## Wool or Felt

Cut out appliqué shapes as described under "Patterns" on the facing page. Pin or baste fabric shapes to your background fabric and blanket stitch around each piece (see "Blanket Stitch" on page 11).

## Cotton Mini-Fuse

In an effort to make cotton appliqué as simple as wool appliqué, I devised a technique called "cotton mini-fuse." It fuses the edges of the cotton appliqué pieces without adding stiffness, and it is easy to stitch through.

Prewash all cotton. Trace the pattern directly from the book onto the top (paper) side of lightweight fusible web.

**1.** Trace the pattern, leaving a generous ½" around it.

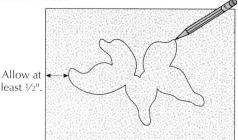

Allow at least ½".

Trace on paper side of fusible web.

> **NOTE:** The finished appliqué piece will be the reverse of what you trace. To correct this, trace the pattern in the book onto tracing paper. Turn the paper over and retrace all lines. Use this side as your pattern and trace onto fusible web. This correction is not necessary if the piece is symmetrical, as with a heart.

**2.** Cut out the center of the traced image ⅛" inside the line as shown. I find that a ⅛" allowance works well for

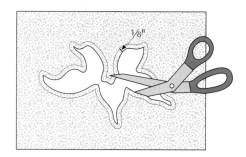

⅛"

Remove inside area.

my blanket stitch. If your blanket stitch is larger, you can leave a wider allowance. I don't recommend cutting any closer than ⅛".

**3.** Fuse the web to the wrong side of the cotton fabric. (Here the need for the generous ½" of web around the tracing becomes obvious. The extra web prevents the pattern from being distorted when fused.)

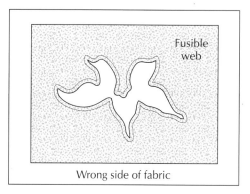

Fusible web

Wrong side of fabric

Fuse.

**4.** Cut out along the traced line. You will be left with a very thin band of web around the perimeter. Remove the paper backing and position the appliqué piece on the background fabric. When all appliqué pieces are in place, fuse.

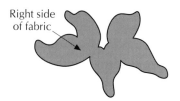

Right side of fabric

Ready to fuse in place

**5.** Blanket stitch around each piece (page 11). As you appliqué, your blanket stitch should straddle the web, so that the needle always goes in and out of plain fabric.

**Cross Section of Cotton Mini-Fuse**

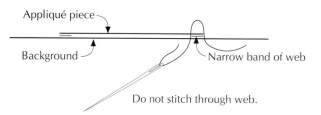

Appliqué piece

Background

Narrow band of web

Do not stitch through web.

# Felt Cutwork

Eastern Europe has an extraordinary needlework and textile heritage. One stunning example of this heritage is felt cutwork. This technique involves machine stitching two contrasting colors of felt together in a decorative design and then cutting away parts of the top layer to reveal the contrasting felt underneath. Two projects in this book were designed specifically for this technique: "… And Eight Tiny Reindeer" (page 50) and "The Birds I" (page 52).

**1.** Trace the stitching design from the book onto the tracing paper, using a dark Pigma pen with a fine point (.01). Layer the tracing paper, background felt, and top or appliqué felt together as shown and pin.

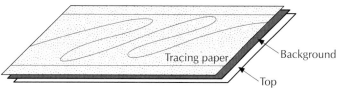
Tracing paper — Background — Top

**2.** Prepare your sewing machine for free-motion quilting. For my somewhat dated machine, that means lowering the feed dogs, releasing all pressure in the presser foot, and setting the stitch length to the shortest stitch possible. I also replace the standard presser foot with the buttonhole foot, since my machine does not have an embroidery or darning foot.

> **NOTE:** Some sewing machines cannot be adjusted for this type of sewing. You can do the project with the machine set up for normal stitching (regular foot, feed dogs up), but you will have to stitch slowly and carefully, especially around curves.

**3.** Thread the machine (top and bobbin) with machine-quilting thread. Because you stitch from the back, the bobbin thread will end up on the front of your runner. Be sure you insert thread of the right color and type.

**4.** Stitch through the tracing paper and 2 layers of felt, following the design drawn on the paper. Gently remove the paper.

**5.** Gather together all of your favorite small, sharp pairs of scissors. A pair with large finger holes is my favorite. You will be doing lots of cutting. Working from the front or top side of your table runner (the opposite side from the one that had the paper), carefully poke the scissors through only the top layer of felt. Cut away sections of the top layer, leaving the background color exposed. Use the color photos (pages 17–32) as a guide.

A pinked edge is very characteristic of this type of work. Pinking shears work on long, straight edges, but are cumbersome in other areas. In small areas and tight curves, you will need to pink the edges with your regular scissors. To do this, first cut around the shape, leaving a generous allowance, then notch out the pinked design. You decide which edges to pink and which to cut straight. The color photos are just a guide. Feel free to create the design that you want.

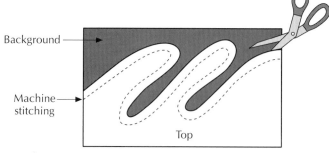
Background — Machine stitching — Top

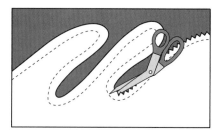
Notch border to make pinked edge.

Top — Pinked edge — Background — Straight-cut edge

# HAND STITCHING

## Blanket Stitch

This is the basic blanket stitch. I use it to appliqué wool, felt, and cotton. Use 2 strands of cotton embroidery floss and a #08 crewel needle.

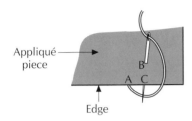

Appliqué piece

Edge

Stitch around each piece. Be sure to catch the appliqué fabric and the background fabric with each stitch.

Keep your stitches loose. If you pull too tightly, the section of thread that lies along the edge of the appliqué piece will disappear under the appliqué. Try to keep your stitch size uniform on each pattern piece. Use longer stitches farther apart for larger pieces, and shorter stitches closer together for smaller pieces as shown.

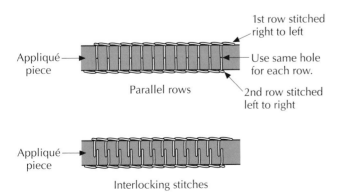

Large piece   Medium piece   Small piece

Two ways to arrange your blanket stitches on narrow or skinny pieces are shown below.

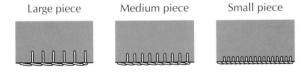

1st row stitched right to left

Appliqué piece

Use same hole for each row.

Parallel rows

2nd row stitched left to right

Appliqué piece

Interlocking stitches

Group several stitches close together at a corner. Many stitches close together tend to lie flatter than an isolated stitch.

## Embroidery

To get the look I want, I do all of my embroidered details with two strands of embroidery floss and a #08 crewel needle. Silk ribbon, crewel yarn, perle cotton, and any other decorative threads are also acceptable.

I most often use the following stitches.

### Blanket Stitch

This is the stitch I use for appliqué, but it can also be used decoratively. See the directions at left.

### Chain Stitch

Use a small stitch to hold the chain in place when changing directions.

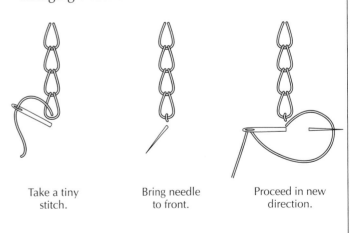

Take a tiny stitch.   Bring needle to front.   Proceed in new direction.

### French Knot

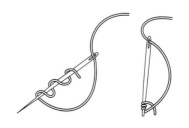

## Lazy Daisy

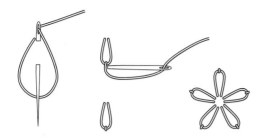

## Feather Stitch

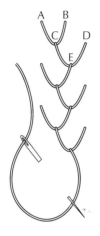

1. Bring the needle up at A, then down at B, forming a U-shape.
2. Bring the needle back up at C to form the "catch," then down at D, once again forming a U-shape.
3. Bring the needle back up at E to catch the U. Continue working to the left and right in this manner.

## Backstitch

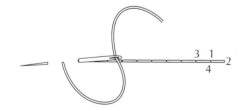

## Cross-Stitch and Star Stitch

Step 1   Step 2        Step 3   Step 4

    Cross-Stitch          Star Stitch

## Running Stitch

This is what I use for my quilting stitch. It is big, bright, and bold.

## Stem Stitch

## Ribbon Stitch

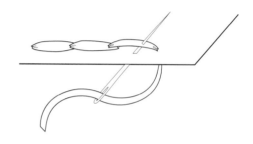

# FINISHING

## *Initialing Your Work*

After all the time and effort you put into your table runner, take a few minutes to sign and date it. My favorite technique is to chain stitch my initials and the year on the front of my work. Also consider adding a label to the back of the piece so you can add even more information for future generations.

*JCB*

## *Choosing Batting*

Batting is optional for the projects in this book. I did use it for the Garden series runners to help support the weight of the buttons. My personal favorite is Hobbs Thermore batting because it is so thin and lightweight.

## Quilting

There are no hard-and-fast rules about quilting a table runner. If quilting enhances the overall look you are after, by all means add it. Since most of the table runners in this book do not call for batting, there is no real reason to quilt—unless you like the look.

## Backing and Binding

For backings and bindings, I use 100%-cotton quilting fabrics. They come in a wonderful variety of colors and prints. Choose a backing and binding that coordinate with each other as well as with the top of the runner.

For most of the table runners in this book, a straight-grain, single-fold binding is all that is needed. If you choose to round off the edges of your runner, you will need a bias binding.

### Making the Binding

To make *straight-grain binding*, cut 1½"-wide strips of fabric, across the width if possible. Stitch strips together end to end (not at an angle) until you have enough to go around the runner. Press seams open.

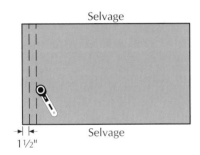

Selvage

Selvage

1½"

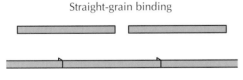

Straight-grain binding

Length = total of all 4 sides of runner
(or circumference) + 10" insurance

To make *bias binding*, start with fat quarters of fabric (18" x 22"). One fat quarter will make about 200" of 1½"-wide binding, plenty for one of the projects in this book. Press the fabric, making sure the edges are on the straight grain (the threads that run parallel to the edge).

**1.** Fold over one corner of the fabric diagonally to find the "true bias" (the line that runs at a 45° angle to the straight grain).

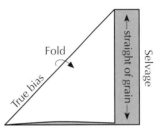

**2.** Cut along this fold line, then use the cut edge as a guide to rotary cut 1½"-wide strips.

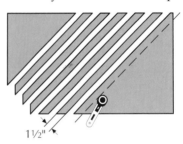

1½"

**3.** Stitch the strips together as shown until you have enough to go around the runner. (See the formula given at lower left.) Press the seams open.

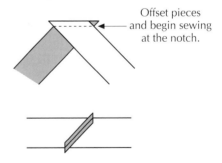

Offset pieces and begin sewing at the notch.

### Attaching the Binding

**1.** With right sides together, line up the raw edges of the binding and the runner top. Fold the beginning of the binding back ½" over itself and pin in place as shown on page 14. Stitch along one side of the runner, using a ¼"-wide seam allowance and stopping ¼" from the edge. Backstitch and clip the threads.

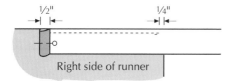
Right side of runner

**2.** Remove the runner from the machine. Fold the binding up and away from the runner so that the outside edge lines up with the next side to be sewn, and the inside edge forms a right angle with the side you just sewed. Now fold it back down along the next side to be sewn, with raw edges even and the fold along the previously sewn (top) edge.

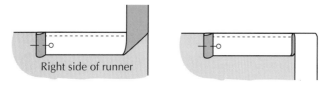
Right side of runner

**3.** Starting at the top, stitch down the next side, stopping ¼" from the next edge. Backstitch.

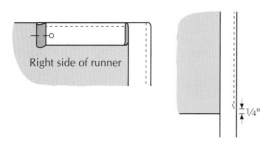
Right side of runner

¼"

**4.** Repeat steps 2 and 3 until you have stitched all the way around the runner. As you reach your starting place, overlap the binding about ¼" over the fold. Trim off the extra binding, then finish stitching the binding to the runner.

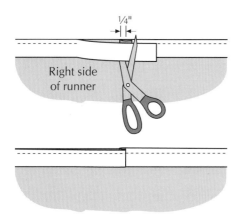
¼"
Right side of runner

**5.** Fold the binding to the back of the runner and turn under ¼" along the raw edge. Pin and slipstitch in place. The hem covers the machine stitching, and miters magically form at the corners.

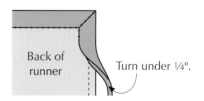
Back of runner
Turn under ¼".

## Tongue Borders

### Wool and Felt Tongue Borders

There are two ways to cut out tongue shapes from wool or felt. The first is to use a paper pattern pinned to the fabric. Patterns are provided at the back of the book. Trace the pattern onto tracing paper and cut out. Pin the tracing-paper pattern to fabric and cut out.

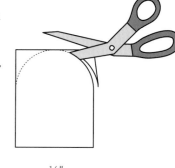

The second is what I refer to as the "freehand" method. Using a rotary cutter, cut rectangles to the size given in the project instructions. To make round tongues, trim corners at one short end in a curve. To make pointed tongues, trim corners at a 45° angle, leaving ¼" between cuts.

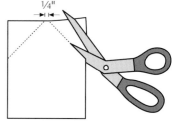
¼"
Eyeball a 45° angle.

For wool, use blanket stitches to finish the rounded edge.

Felt edges can be left plain, finished with a blanket stitch, or given a decorative edge with pinking or scalloping shears.

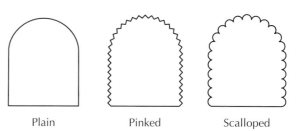
Plain
Pinked
Scalloped

## Cotton Tongue Borders

**1.** Rotary cut cotton squares or rectangles according to the project instructions. With right sides together, layer the tongue fronts and tongue backs.

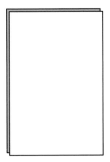

Place 2 cotton rectangles
right sides together.

**2.** Cut rounded corners at one end of each pair. You can cut freehand or use the patterns provided at the back of the book.

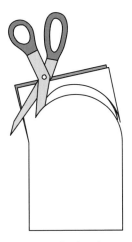

Cut freehand or
pin pattern in place.

**3.** Sew around the long, curved edge of each pair, using a ¼"-wide seam allowance. Stitch again just inside the previous stitching. Trim as shown.

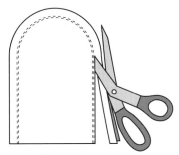

Double stitch a ¼"-wide seam allowance;
trim close to stitches.

**4.** Turn the tongues right side out and press.

**5.** To attach tongue borders to the runner, follow the directions given for each project.

> **Note:** Cotton tongue borders require more than twice as much fabric as wool or felt tongue borders. To convert a wool or felt project to cotton, double the number of rectangles and add ½" to the width and ¼" to the length of each for seam allowances. So if a wool project calls for 12 tongues, each 2" x 3¾", you will need 24 cotton tongues, each 2½" x 4".

# MY VALENTINE

**Finished Size (including tongue border): 13" x 41"**

*Color photo on facing page*

Hearts and birds are universal images of love. Cultures and religions the world over honor the heart as a life-giving force and revere birds as the go-betweens of heaven and earth. The following directions are for the red-and-white wool-on-wool runner pictured in the top photo on the facing page. To duplicate the cotton runner shown in the bottom photo, use a variety of pink prints on a red cotton background. Instructions for cotton appliqué are on page 9. The cotton version is finished with a scrap binding (see pages 13–14).

## MATERIALS

*Yardage is based on 60"-wide wool and 44"-wide cotton. Adjust the yardage amounts if you change the size to fit your table.*

½ yd. or a 13½" x 34½" piece of white wool for background

½ yd. red wool for appliqué and tongues

½ yd. cotton fabric for backing

White embroidery floss

## CUTTING

*Use the patterns on pages 59–60.*
From the white wool, cut:
    1 piece, 13½" x 34½", for background

From the red wool, cut:
    4 birds (2 and 2 reversed)

    2 large hearts

    2 medium hearts

    18 small hearts

    3 circles, each 1⅛" in diameter

    12 tongues, each 2" x 3¾" (Round off corners, either freehand or using the pattern provided on page 96.)

From the cotton fabric, cut:
    1 piece, 13½" x 34½", for backing

## ASSEMBLY

**1.** Fold the background fabric in half lengthwise and crosswise. Press. Open out. The creases will help you center your design. Arrange all of the appliqué pieces on the background fabric, using the illustration above as a guide. Pin or baste, then blanket stitch around each piece, using white embroidery floss (see page 11).

**2.** Blanket stitch the long curved edge of each wool or felt tongue, or follow the directions for cotton tongues on page 15.

*continued on page 33*

*MY VALENTINE, above, by Janet Carija Brandt, 1998, Indianapolis, Indiana, 13" x 41"; wool. Why limit a table runner to the dining room? This traditional folk-art runner is draped over a nightstand, providing warmth and charm by a cozy bedside.*

*BE MY VALENTINE by Janet Carija Brandt, 1998, Indianapolis, Indiana, 17½" x 32"; cotton appliqué. Made by Debby Eads, Indianapolis, Indiana. Easily hung with a simple cafe curtain rod and clips, this runner features bird and heart shapes in pretty pinks and reds, adding character to this red room. Use this decorating idea with any of the longer, thinner runners in the book for a dramatic window treatment.*

*MY SUMMER GARDEN* by Janet Carija Brandt, 1998, Indianapolis, Indiana, 15" x 49"; cotton and buttons. Polish your outdoor decor with this summertime runner, placed outside on a wicker tabletop. The brightly colored buttons create a towering field of summer flowers against a cheerful patchwork border.

*LITTLE TEAPOTS* (facing page), by Janet Carija Brandt, 1998, Indianapolis, Indiana, 25½" x 44"; embroidery on cotton. Made by Debby Eads, Indianapolis, Indiana. Refine an otherwise plain tabletop with these embroidered teapot figures, taken from "I'm a Little Teapot." Use for more casual indoor and outdoor dining.

*I'M A LITTLE TEAPOT* by Janet Carija Brandt, 1998, Indianapolis, Indiana, 17" x 49"; felt on cotton. Perfect for a morning or afternoon get-together with friends, these vivid blue figurines on a delicately striped background add a fresh presentation to any table, whether special occasion or everyday.

*. . . AND EIGHT TINY REINDEER by Janet Carija Brandt, 1998, Indianapolis, Indiana, 12" x 66"; felt. Santa and his galloping gang lend a touch of whimsy to this traditional Christmas mantel. Add fresh holly sprigs and your favorite holiday knickknacks for an impressive focal point in a formal or informal living space.*

*SNOWFLAKES (facing page), by Janet Carija Brandt, 1998, Indianapolis, Indiana, 9¼" x 74½"; cotton appliqué with rayon fringe. Toast the holidays and the coming new year with this crisp wintertime runner, reminiscent of a shimmery, snow-flaked twilight sky. Along a table or bar, it's the perfect accent to your most elegant and sophisticated holiday event. The fringed edges add just the right amount of holiday sparkle.*

*SANTA IN HIS SLEIGH by Janet Carija Brandt, 1998, Indianapolis, Indiana, 16" x 29"; felt. Made by Brian Haggard, Greenwood, Indiana. A delightful pinked and curved border complements this smaller version of ". . . And Eight Tiny Reindeer" (above). The glittery gold polka dots invite merriment to this holiday table. Try draping this runner over furniture or hanging it on a wall in a room that needs some extra Christmas cheer.*

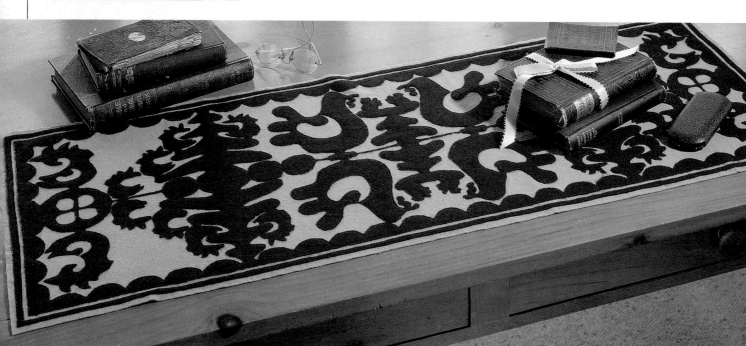

*SPRING GARDEN* by Janet Carija Brandt, 1998, Indianapolis, Indiana, 15" x 40½"; cotton, buttons, and silk ribbon. Throw a delectable tea-and-cake party with this delicate design as your centerpiece. Filled with buttons and tied silk ribbons, this runner is nicely framed by a pretty pastel patchwork border.

*Try placing "Spring Garden" on a dressing table to coax springtime into a private bedroom or bath.*

*LITTLE BIRDS* by Janet Carija Brandt, 1998, Indianapolis, Indiana, 15½" x 41"; felt cutwork. Made by Jan Paul, Indianapolis, Indiana. The deep, rich colors of this design can complement a more masculine decor.

*THE BIRDS I by Janet Carija Brandt, 1998, Indianapolis, Indiana, 15½" x 41"; felt. Made by Brian Haggard, Greenwood, Indiana. Add an appealing folk-art touch to your next family gathering with this elaborate, yet charming felt cutwork runner.*

*THE BIRDS II by Janet Carija Brandt, 1998, Indianapolis, Indiana, 25" x 25"; wool and ribbon. Janet converted the design elements of "The Birds I" (page 23) into shapes for traditional appliqué. Bright colors splash from a solid background to create a wonderful everyday wool-on-wool design. Use it between holidays and other special events to keep color in your decor.*

*HAPPY BIRTHDAY, LITTLE BEAR! by Janet Carija Brandt, 1998, Indianapolis, Indiana, 14" x 41"; cotton. Let the festivities begin! Children love this irresistible scene of animals gathering to celebrate a birthday. Make this runner a family tradition.*

*JANE SAYS THERE SHOULD BE FISH* by Janet Carija Brandt, 1998, Indianapolis, Indiana, 15" x 49"; cotton, buttons, beads, and silk ribbon. Hues of ocean blue and seafoam green highlight this enchanting underwater scene. For fun, use this piece to embellish a summertime buffet or picnic table.

Detail (inset facing page) of "Jane Says There Should Be Fish." Tiny green fish swimming along the runner seem to gently sway the quilted waves and silk-ribbon foliage.

*HARVEST WALTZ I by Janet Carija Brandt, 1997, Indianapolis, Indiana, 16" x 85"; embroidery, beads, and bells on cotton. For embroidery enthusiasts, this runner is a wonderful alternative to appliqué—Janet simply reversed the design. Whether in a dining room, den, or hallway, this harvest scene will carry your decor from the first signs of autumn to the unpacking of Christmas decorations.*

*HARVEST WALTZ II by Janet Carija Brandt, 1998, Indianapolis, Indiana, 18" x 60"; cotton. This festive autumn scene features characters dancing in the pumpkin patch by moonlight. Here, the runner accents a hall table, but it could pull together an autumn decor in any area of your home.*

*Detail of "Harvest Waltz I." The beads-and-bells border adds flair and creates a gentle chime for passersby.*

**AUTUMN TREE OF LIFE** *by Janet Carija Brandt, 1998,
Indianapolis, Indiana, 17" x 42"; wool-on-wool appliqué. Made by
Debra Haggard, Greenwood, Indiana. This classic folk art–style
runner showcases the soft, soothing colors of autumn on this
natural-wood kitchen table. Add a spray of dried fall flowers for a
casual, yet finished look.*

*Detail of "Autumn Tree of Life".
The simple circles, hearts,
harvest moons, and figures
add texture and dimension to
this design. The golden star
atop the tree completes the
primitive scene.*

**AUTUMN GARDEN** *(below) by Janet Carija Brandt, 1998, Indianapolis,
Indiana, 15" x 49"; cotton and buttons, with loosely woven wool for trees.
Made by Debra Haggard, Greenwood, Indiana. We've added a homemade
wooden birdhouse to this rich, whimsical forest landscape. Falling leaves
are represented by an array of colorful buttons. The bright patchwork
border adds just the right splash of color to this countertop.*

*TREE OF LIFE by Janet Carija Brandt, 1998, Indianapolis, Indiana, 19" x 59"; felt appliqué on cotton towels. Made by Suzanne Marie Borse, Indianapolis, Indiana. This variation on "Autumn Tree of Life" (facing page, top) is an extra-easy way to adorn a table. The calm, soothing neutral hues give an illusion of spaciousness.*

Detail of "Tree of Life." The simple, thin lines on the purchased cotton towels add a sophisticated accent to this primitive appliquéd scene—and provide a handy placement guide, too!

Try draping a runner over a sofa back, as with "Easter Baskets" above, then accent your creation with coordinating stuffed animals and pillows.

*EASTER BASKETS* by *Janet Carija Brandt, 1998, Indianapolis, Indiana, 15" x 46"; wool. Position this pretty Easter runner along any surface that needs a burst of springtime color. Interwoven strips of wool make a wonderfully textured basket for the pastel eggs.*

*continued from page 16*

**3.** Place 6 tongues along each end of the table runner with right sides together and raw edges even. Baste.

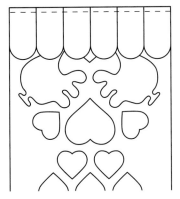

Baste tongues to end of runner.

**4.** With right sides together, sew the runner to the backing fabric, leaving a small opening on one side. Turn right side out. Slipstitch the opening closed. Press. Blanket stitch along each long edge.

**5.** Sign and date your table runner.

## DESIGN OPTIONS

➤ Add or subtract birds or hearts (or both) to adjust this design to fit any size runner. Try lengthening the design by adding elements that will hang over the ends of the table.

➤ Try narrowing the design by lining up hearts and birds along the edges.

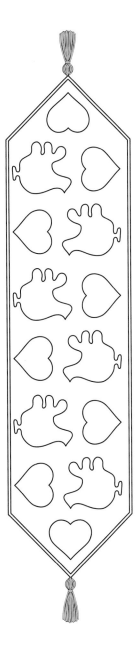

# EASTER BASKETS

**Finished Size: 15" x 46"**

*Color photo on page 32*

Nothing says Easter like a woven basket filled with colored eggs and a vast field of pretty blooms. While the soft colors and texture of wool make the runner shown on page 32 especially appealing, you could use any fabric. Fabric requirements are the same no matter what fabric you use.

## MATERIALS

*Yardage is based on 60"-wide wool and 44"-wide cotton. Adjust the yardage amounts if you change the size to fit your table.*

⅝ yd. or a 15" x 46" piece of off-white wool for background

6 assorted pastel wools, each 14" x 14", for appliqué

¾ yd. cotton fabric for backing (1½ yds. for unpieced backing)

¼ yd. cotton fabric for binding

Embroidery floss to match the assorted wool colors

## CUTTING

*Use the patterns on page 61.*

From the off-white wool, cut a 15" x 46" piece for the background.

From the assorted pastel wools, choose your basket color and cut out the vertical basket strips and basket base first, using the patterns.

For the horizontal strips, cut:

2 strips, each ½" x 6½"

2 strips, each ½" x 5¾"

2 strips, each ½" x 5"

2 strips, each ½" x 4½"

2 strips, each ½" x 4¼"

Cut 4 eggs *each* from 4 of your colors and 3 eggs *each* from the remaining 2 colors for a total of *22*.

From the remaining appliqué fabrics, cut out an assortment of flowers and leaves. You will need approximately 42 large flowers, 32 medium flowers, and 52 small flowers. You will also need 30 large leaves and 9 small leaves. Use the patterns provided for most of the pieces, then cut the scraps into odd-size flowers and leaves.

For a pieced backing, cut a 15" strip across the width of the backing fabric. Cut a 15"-wide piece from the remaining fabric; join it to one end of the crosswise strip, using a ¼" seam allowance. Press the seam open. Trim the resulting piece to 15" x 46".

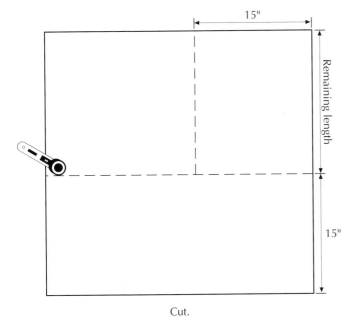

Cut.

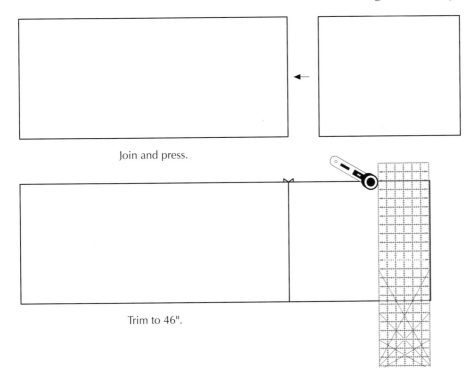

Join and press.

Trim to 46".

For an unpieced backing, cut a 15" x 46" piece from the length of the backing fabric.

From the binding fabric, cut and piece 1½"-wide crosswise strips until you have a strip at least 132" long for binding (see page 13).

## ASSEMBLY

**1.** Arrange the baskets and eggs on the background fabric, using the photo on page 32 and the illustration opposite as a guide. Slip a few eggs under the top edge of the basket. Pin or baste, then blanket stitch everything in place with matching embroidery floss.

**2.** Divide your pile of flowers and leaves in half. Place half along one side and the other half along the other side, using the color photo as a guide. Blanket stitch in place.

**3.** Lay the runner on the backing fabric with wrong sides together. Bind the edges (see pages 13–14).

**4.** Sign and date your table runner.

# DESIGN OPTIONS

➤ This design is easy to adapt to any length of table. Simply add or eliminate flowers to lengthen or shorten the runner.

➤ Center one basket of flowers on an oval runner and surround it with a wreath of flowers.

➤ Eliminate the baskets of eggs and make a runner of just flowers. If you are feeling really fancy, cut the edge of the runner to echo the curves of the flowers. Don't try to bind that edge. Instead, sew the backing to the runner with right sides together, leaving a small opening. Clip the curves and turn right side out. Slipstitch the opening closed and, if you like, blanket stitch the edge.

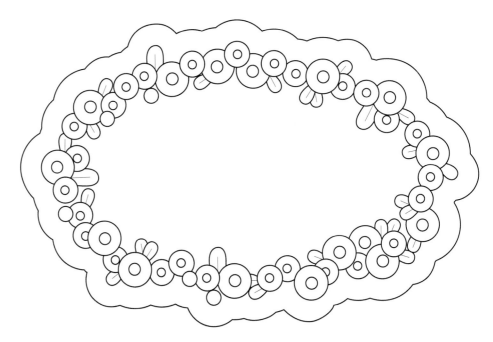

# MY SUMMER GARDEN

**Finished Size: 15" x 49"**

*Color photo on page 18*

When my children were very little and I needed a few moments of quiet time, I escaped to my "garden." It was a four-foot by twenty-foot border next to a chain-link fence—my own little Eden. Pulling weeds was pure joy.

My kids are quite a bit older now, and I enjoy every minute that they can spare for good ol' Mom. Unfortunately, as my kids and the garden have grown, the time I am willing to devote to weeding has shrunk.

Here is the perfect garden. It never needs weeding or watering, and it blooms continuously.

## MATERIALS

*Yardage is based on 44"-wide cotton fabric. Adjust the yardage amounts if you change the size to fit your table.*

1⅝ yds. deep yellow for background

8 assorted bright solid fat eighths for checkerboard border (use more colors if you like)

⅞ yd. for pieced backing (1⅝ yds. for unpieced backing)

¼ yd. royal blue for binding

17" x 51" piece of lightweight batting (supports the weight of the buttons)

Approximately 200 assorted buttons

Embroidery floss to match buttons and in various shades of green for stems

Silk ribbon for stems (optional)

## CUTTING

From the yellow fabric, cut an 11½" x 45½" piece for the background.

From each of the 8 fat eighths, cut 4 strips, each 1½" x 13½", for a total of 32. (You will use 30.)

For a pieced backing, cut a 17" strip across the width of the backing fabric. Cut a 17"-wide piece from the remaining fabric; join it to one end of the crosswise strip, using a ¼" seam allowance. Press the seam open. Trim the resulting piece to 17" x 51".

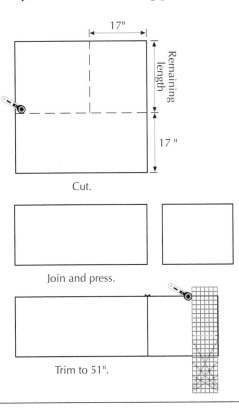

Cut.

Join and press.

Trim to 51".

For an unpieced backing, cut a 17" x 51" piece from the length of the backing fabric.

From the royal blue fabric, cut and piece 1½"-wide crosswise strips until you have a strip at least 138" long for binding (see page 13).

## ASSEMBLY

### Checkerboard Border

**1.** Randomly piece together 15 of the 13½" strips as shown. Use a ¼" seam allowance. Press the seam allowances to one side. Make 2 strip sets.

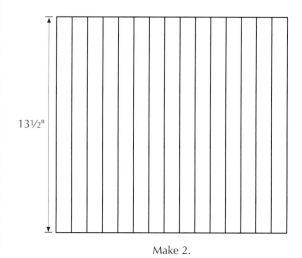

13½"

Make 2.

**2.** Trim the top edge, then crosscut each strip set into 8 pieced units, each 1½" wide. You will have a total of 16 pieced units.

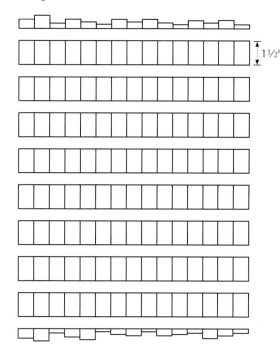

1½"

**3.** Randomly choose 3 units and connect them end to end to make a long piece with 45 tiny rectangles. Press. Make 4 long pieces.

Make 4.

**4.** Join 2 of these long strips along the long edges as shown. Press. Join the other 2 in a similar fashion. These will form the top and bottom borders.

Make 2.

**5.** Using the 4 remaining pieced units from step 2, join 2 units to make a side border. Repeat for the other side border. Press.

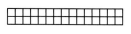

Make 2.

**6.** Stitch the long borders to the top and bottom of the background fabric. Press the seam allowances toward the border.

Background fabric

**7.** Stitch the short borders to either side of the background fabric. Press.

## Garden

Now to make your garden grow!

**1.** Spread the background out on a tabletop and play with possible button arrangements. When you are happy with the design, make some quick notes and sketches so you remember what you had in mind. Like a real garden, this design will evolve as you work.

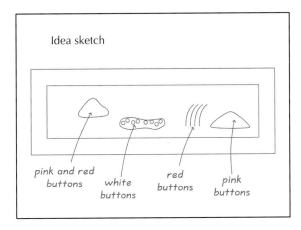

Idea sketch

pink and red buttons

white buttons

red buttons

pink buttons

**2.** Work with 1 color group at a time. Using 3 strands of embroidery floss, stitch the buttons in place. I started with purple buttons on the lower right side.

**3.** As you move from one button group to the next, stand back every now and then and look at your runner from a distance to see how the overall composition is coming along. Leave some open space where vases, dishes, and candlesticks can be set on a smooth surface. You don't want things tipping over and spilling on your beautiful work.

**4.** When all your buttons have been sewn in place, add embroidered stems using the floss or silk ribbon. Use a variety of stitches (see pages 11–12). Don't worry about making a stem for every single button. Just as in a real garden, you can't and don't need to see all of the stems at one time.

**5.** Layer the runner with backing and batting as you would a quilt. Quilt sparsely by hand or machine, just enough to suggest busy bees hopping from flower to flower.

**6.** Trim the backing and batting even with the edges of the runner top.

**7.** Bind the edges (see pages 13–14).

**8.** Sign and date your table runner.

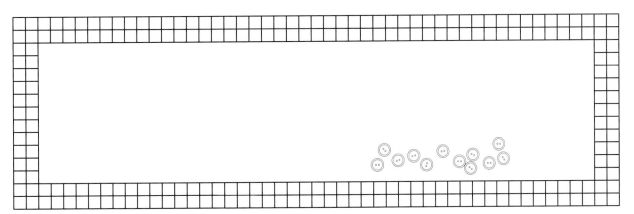

Randomly sew on one color at a time.

# DESIGN OPTIONS

➤ This table runner can be made any size, but because of the checkerboard border, it must have straight sides (no circles or ovals). Try a long, narrow runner for a sofa table. Fill it with tiny violets and spring beauties amid the blades of grass.

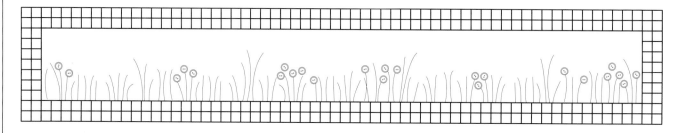

➤ Make a square cover for a bedside table. Let the flowers bloom on all four sides.

➤ Be sure to check out the spring, water-garden, and autumn variations of this runner on pages 22, 26–27, and 30.

# I'M A LITTLE TEAPOT

**Finished Size (including tongue border): 17" x 49"**

*Color photo on page 18*

*I'm a little teapot, short and stout,*
*Here is my handle, here is my spout,*
*When I get all steamed up, then I shout,*
*Just tip me over and pour me out.*

This children's rhyme is filled with wonderful imagery. The appliquéd runner on page 18 was made with a cotton background and backing. Felt was used for the appliqué pieces and tongue border.

## MATERIALS

*Yardage is based on 44"-wide cotton and 60"-wide wool felt. Please read about felt on page 7. Adjust the yardage amounts if you change the size to fit your table.*

¾ yd. white cotton fabric for background and binding

⅝ yd. blue felt for teapots, teacups, saucers, teaspoons, leaves, and tongues

9" x 12" piece of white felt for aprons, faces, and flowers

Scrap of yellow felt for flower centers and dress ornaments

⅝ yd. cotton fabric for backing

White and blue embroidery floss

## CUTTING

*Use the patterns on pages 62 –65.*
From the white cotton, cut:

1 piece, 17" x 38", for the background. Cut and piece 1½"-wide crosswise strips until you have a strip at least 120" long for binding (see page 13).

From the blue felt, cut:

2 of each teapot design (6 teapots total)

2 of each teacup design (6 teacups total)

2 of each saucer design (6 saucers total)

3 teaspoons

15 leaves

4 small dots for flowers on Teapot 1 apron

16 tongues, each 2" x 6". Cut off 2 corners to form a point, either freehand or using the pattern provided on page 96.

**Note:** *Teapot 1 has a separate hair/hat section. On Teapots 2 and 3, cut out face area along solid line.*

From the white felt, cut:

Faces and aprons for teapots

8 small dots for bottom of Teapot 2 dresses and flowers on Teapot 1 apron

16 tiny dots for Teapot 2 dresses

9 flowers

*Note: The faces will lie under the blue areas. Cut out to the dashed line. The aprons will lie on top of the blue areas. On Teapot 3, cut out the bodice/apron as one piece.*

From the yellow felt, cut:
    13 small dots for flower centers and flowers on Teapot 1 apron

From the backing fabric, cut:
    1 piece, 17" x 38"

### ASSEMBLY

**1.** Assemble and embellish teapots *before* you sew them to the background. Add appliquéd faces, aprons, bodices, dots, and decorative embroidery, using the appliqué patterns as guides. Remember to place the faces under the surrounding blue areas.

**2.** Embroider the teacup rims and saucer centers; attach the flower centers.

**3.** Arrange all of the design elements on the background fabric. Pin or baste. Using embroidery floss, blanket stitch in place. Use the star stitch (see page 12) in the dot centers to secure the flowers.

**4.** Lay the runner on the backing fabric with wrong sides together. Bind the edges (see pages 13–14).

**5.** Arrange 8 tongues on each end of the runner. Slipstitch to the back edge of the runner, lining up the edges of the tongues with the inner edge of the binding.

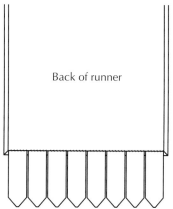

Back of runner

**6.** Sign and date your table runner.

### DESIGN OPTIONS

➤   Just as you might line a shelf with a teapot collection, line a long runner with a colorful collection of these short and stout teapots.

➤   Any one of these teapot designs could be appliquéd to a tea cozy.

The runner in the photo on page 19 is all embroidery, with an extra-wide border. To transfer the design, use a light table or a window. Place the background fabric over the design and trace with a fine-point Pigma pen.

# AUTUMN TREE OF LIFE

**Finished Size: 17" x 42"**

*Color photo on page 30*

There are as many versions of the Tree of Life as there are people drawing it. It seems to be a universal image; almost every culture has an interpretation. Use this design as is or feel free to adapt the figures to suit the story you want to tell. The following directions are for a wool-on-wool version done in warm earth tones.

## MATERIALS

*Yardage is based on 60"-wide wool and 44"-wide cotton. Adjust the yardage amounts if you change the size to fit your table.*

⅝ yd. dark brown wool for background

16" x 18" piece of light brown wool for tree trunk and branches

8" x 16" piece of pale yellow wool for animals, moons, and star

4 assorted wool colors, each 8" x 8", for hearts, fruits, and leaves

6" x 6" piece of pale blue wool for shirt and dress

Tiny darker blue wool scrap for man's pants

Tiny wool scraps for faces

⅝ yd. cotton fabric for backing

1 fat quarter of tan cotton fabric for bias binding

Embroidery floss to match the wool colors

## CUTTING

*Use the patterns on pages 66–70.*

From the dark brown wool, cut a 17" x 42" piece for background.

From the wool fabrics, cut out the appliqué pieces.

From the ⅝ yard of cotton fabric, cut a 17" x 42" piece for the backing.

From the fat quarter of cotton fabric, cut and piece 1½"-wide bias strips until you have a strip at least 128" long for binding (see page 13).

## ASSEMBLY

**1.** Bring the short ends of the background fabric together and lightly press along the fold to mark the center. Arrange the tree trunk and branches on the background fabric and pin or baste. Using matching embroidery floss, appliqué with a blanket stitch.

**2.** Arrange the hearts, fruits, and leaves on the branches. Pin or baste. Blanket stitch in place. The fruit on the bottom branch is connected to the branch with little chain-stitched stems (see page 11).

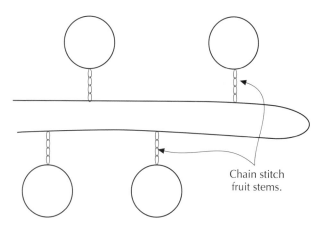

Chain stitch fruit stems.

**3.** Embroider the woman's vest and hem decoration, man's belt, and all facial features. Pin or baste the man and woman in place, tucking faces under clothes. Appliqué with a blanket stitch. Following the pattern, embroider the hair, shoes, and hands.

**4.** Pin or baste the animals and moons in place. Appliqué with a blanket stitch. Add embroidered details as shown on the patterns. Appliqué the star with a chain stitch applied just inside the edges (see photo).

**5.** Lay the runner on the backing fabric with wrong sides together. Round off the corners, either freehand or using the pattern provided.

**6.** Bind the runner (see pages 13–14).

**7.** Sign and date your table runner.

## DESIGN OPTIONS

➤ Check out the "Tree of Life" on page 31 to see how two pretty kitchen towels were sewn together to make a background for this pattern.

➤ Make your Tree of Life into a family tree. Repeat the male and female figures as needed and embroider family names on them.

# HARVEST WALTZ II

**Finished Size: 18" x 60"**

*Color photo on pages 28–29*

I originally designed this merry harvest scene as a rug-hooking pattern. It never got hooked. Now I can finally enjoy my motley crew of moonlighters whenever I like. The runner on pages 28–29 is made from cotton, and the following directions are for the "Cotton Mini-Fuse" technique on page 9. The design would be equally effective in wool or felt.

## MATERIALS

*Yardage is based on 44"-wide cotton fabric. Adjust the yardage amounts if you change the size to fit your table.*

1 yd. medium blue solid for background

10 fat quarters in assorted solids for appliqué pieces and tongues

1¼ yds. for pieced backing (or 1⅞ yds. for unpieced backing)

Lightweight fusible web (omit for wool or felt)

Embroidery floss to match appliqué pieces

## CUTTING

*Use the patterns on pages 70–79.*

From the medium blue fabric, cut 1 piece, 18½" x 40½", for the background and 10 pieces, each 2½" x 18½", for the tongue border.

From the assorted fat quarters, cut out and prepare the appliqué pieces, following the directions for "Cotton Mini-Fuse" on page 9. Remember to reverse the patterns in the book (see page 8).

From the remaining assorted fabrics, cut 172 tongues, each 2½" x 3½". Round off corners, either freehand or using the pattern provided on page 96.

For a pieced backing, cut 2 strips, each 18½" wide, across the width of the backing fabric. Join the strips end to end, using a ¼"-wide seam allowance. Press the seam open. Trim the resulting piece to 18½" x 58½".

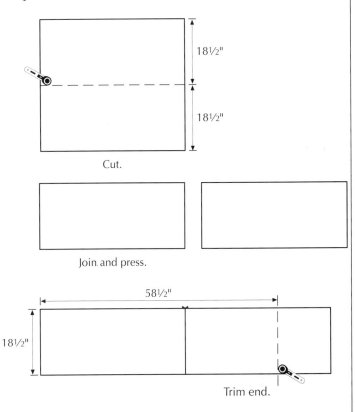

18½"

18½"

Cut.

Join and press.

58½"

18½"

Trim end.

For an unpieced backing, cut an 18½" x 58½" piece from the length of the backing fabric.

## ASSEMBLY

**1.** Arrange all pieces on the background. Take your time and make sure the composition is just what you want. When you are pleased with the arrangement, fuse. Be sure to follow the manufacturer's instructions.

**2.** Using matching embroidery floss, outline each piece with blanket stitches. Embroider the details, following the guides on the pattern for placement.

**3.** Add a horizon by drawing a straight line across the background. Be sure to leave room for the moon. (My horizon runs across my figures at about shoulder height.) Stem stitch over this line (see page 12).

**4.** Trace the moon (page 70) and cut around your tracing. Lay the pattern on the runner in the desired position. Mark around it and embroider. To create the illusion of a rising or setting moon, have only part of the moon showing above the horizon.

**5.** To make cotton tongues, randomly pair up assorted tongue pieces. You should have a total of 86 pairs. Stitch, following the directions on page 15. Blanket stitch the long curved edge of each.

**6.** To make the tongue border:

**a.** Lay a blue border strip, right side up, on your work surface. Place 9 tongues on it as shown. Have raw edges even and leave ¼" of the blue showing at each end. Baste. Repeat to make a total of 6 strips.

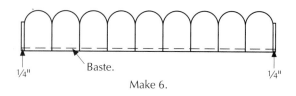

¼"  Baste.  ¼"

Make 6.

**b.** Baste 8 tongues to one of the remaining blue border strips in the same manner, leaving 1¼"

showing at each end. Repeat to make a total of 4 strips.

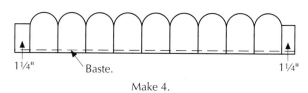

1¼"  Baste.  1¼"

Make 4.

**c.** Place a row of 9 tongues from step *a* on one end of the background fabric with right sides together, raw edges even, and the rounded ends of the tongues pointing toward the appliqué. Stitch. Press the seam allowances toward the runner.

**d.** Add a row with 8 tongues from step *b*. As you add each row, move the tongues from the previous row out of the way so they don't get caught in the seam. Add 3 more rows (9-8-9) to finish this end.

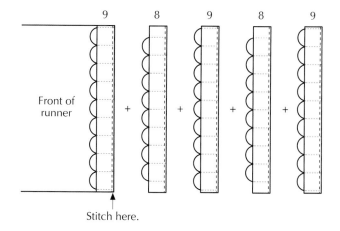

9    8    9    8    9

Front of runner    +    +    +    +

Stitch here.

**e.** Repeat steps *c* and *d* at the other end of the runner.

**7.** With right sides together, stitch the backing fabric to the background fabric, using a ¼"-wide seam allowance; be careful not to catch any tongues in the seam. Leave a small opening at one end of the runner. Turn the runner right side out through the opening. Slipstitch the opening closed. Press.

**8.** Sign and date your table runner.

# DESIGN OPTIONS

➤ This design is easily translated to embroidery. See page 28 for an example. For a smaller design, consider working with fewer figures, perhaps two on each end.

➤ Surround one pair of figures with several rounds of tongues.

# SNOWFLAKES

**Finished Size (including fringe): 9¼" x 74½"**

*Color photo on page 20*

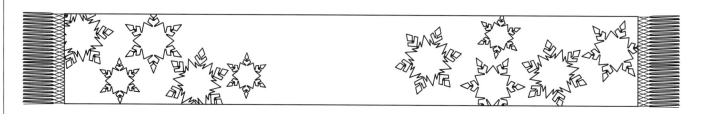

Snow seems to be one of those subjects that people have very strong feelings about. They either love the stuff or hate it. I love snow—it's the ice, cold, and gloom that come with winter that I'm not crazy about. Here are snowflakes that should delight everyone, even a desert dweller. The blue-and-white runner in the photo was made from cotton with a lustrous rayon fringe. The following directions are for the "Cotton Mini-Fuse" technique on page 9.

## MATERIALS

*Yardage is based on 44"-wide cotton fabric. Adjust the yardage amounts if you change the size to fit your table.*

2 yds. blue for background

¾ yd. white for appliqué pieces

¾ yd. for backing

Lightweight fusible web (omit for wool or felt)

White embroidery floss

10 skeins of rayon floss in coordinating colors for fringe

Fray Check or similar product

## CUTTING

*Use the patterns on pages 80–81.*

From the blue fabric, cut a 9¾" x 61½" piece.

From the white fabric, cut out and prepare the snowflake appliqué pieces, following the directions for "Cotton Mini-Fuse" on page 9. The runner on page 20 has 4 large snowflakes, 3 medium

snowflakes, and 3 small snowflakes. Since these patterns are symmetrical, there is no need to reverse them.

From the backing fabric, cut 2 strips, each 9¾" wide, across the width of the fabric. Join the strips end to end, using a ¼"-wide seam allowance. Press the seam open. Trim the resulting piece to 9¾" x 61½".

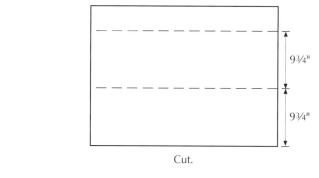

Cut.

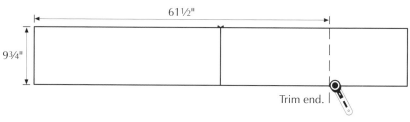

61½"

9¾"

Trim end.

## ASSEMBLY

**1.** Arrange the snowflakes on the background fabric, using the illustration above as a guide. Place some snowflakes so they extend over the edges of the background fabric. Don't trim them until after they are fused. When you are satisfied with the arrangement, fuse. Follow the manufacturer's instructions and be careful not to fuse the over-hanging snowflakes to your ironing board! Trim.

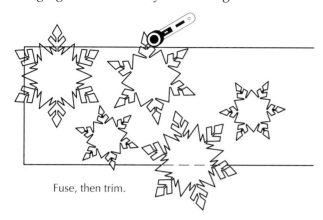

Fuse, then trim.

**2.** Blanket stitch the snowflakes to the background (see page 11).

**3.** With right sides together, sew the background fabric to the backing fabric, using a ¼"-wide seam allowance. Leave a small opening at one end. Turn the runner right side out through the opening. Slipstitch the opening closed. Press.

**4.** Work a blanket stitch along each short end of the runner. This will be your foundation for the fringe. My stitches are approximately ¼" apart.

**5.** To make the fringe:

**a.** Cut the rayon floss into 15" lengths. An easy way to do this is to cut a piece of cardboard 7½" wide by any length. Wrap the floss around the 7½" dimension of the board. Cut along one end.

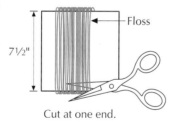

7½"

Floss

Cut at one end.

**b.** Loop 2 strands of the rayon floss through the base of each blanket stitch. This thread is very slippery! I used a *tiny* dab of Fray Check on each loop or knot to hold it in place.

Loop through blanket stitch.

**c.** Divide the fringe and make a row of overhand knots as shown. Seal each knot.

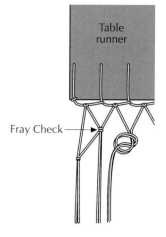

Table runner

Fray Check

**d.** Divide, knot, and seal again.

**e.** Repeat steps *b–d* on the other end of the runner.

**6.** Sign and date your table runner.

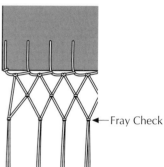

Fray Check

## DESIGN OPTIONS

➢ An elegant option for this runner would be a white-on-white color scheme with a beaded edge. String the beads to look like shiny icicles hanging over your table's edge.

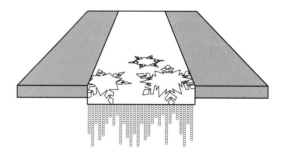

➢ For a tiny tabletop, leave the top blank and let the snowflakes and border cascade down either side.

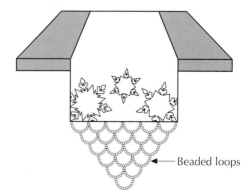

Beaded loops

# ... AND EIGHT TINY REINDEER

**Finished Size: 12" x 66"**

*Color photo on page 21*

*W*hen, what to my wondering eyes should appear,
    But a miniature sleigh and eight tiny reindeer,
With a little old driver so lively and quick,
I knew in a moment it must be Saint Nick.
More rapid than eagles his coursers they came,
And he whistled and shouted and called them by name:
"Now, Dasher! Now, Dancer! Now, Prancer and Vixen!
On, Comet! On, Cupid! On, Donner and Blitzen!"

From *The Night Before Christmas*
by Clement C. Moore

This is a felt cutwork runner. Refer to the directions on page 10.

## MATERIALS

*Yardage is based on 60"-wide wool felt. Adjust the amounts if you change the size to fit your table.*

2 yds. or one 14" x 68" piece of red felt for background

2 yds. or one 14" x 68" piece of white felt for top

18"-wide tracing paper

Size .01 Pigma pen

White machine-quilting thread

#16 sewing-machine needle

## CUTTING

From the background fabric, cut a 14" x 68" piece. From the top fabric, cut a 14" x 68" piece.

## ASSEMBLY

*Use the patterns on pages 82–84.*

**1.** Using the Pigma pen, make a full-size drawing of Santa and 8 reindeer on the tracing paper. Be sure to draw the straight outside borders, too (see facing page, top). The tracing paper is your stitching guide.

**2.** Layer the tracing paper with the background and top as shown in the diagram on page 10. Pin.

**3.** Thread the machine (top and bobbin) with the white quilting thread and use the #16 needle.

## TIP

The design is drawn in two lines, each of which can be sewn without a break, similar to a machine-quilting design. Stitch the Santa/reindeer/tree line, then stitch the collar/rein line. Trace over each line with your finger before you begin, to get a feel for the direction the stitching will follow.

Stitch reindeer . . .      . . . then stitch reins and collar.

Stitch the borders first. This will keep the tracing paper in place for the next step. The paper may wrinkle and crease, but a little wrinkling is okay.

Paper wrinkles

Stitch borders first.

½"

¼"

½"

**4.** Adjust your sewing machine for free-motion quilting (see page 10). Before you begin stitching, pull the bobbin thread up to the paper side. Stitch over all the traced lines. Tear away the tracing paper when the stitching is complete.

**5.** Cut away the top felt, following the directions on page 10. In the photo on page 21, only the tree and border outlines are pinked.

**6.** Sign and date your table runner.

## DESIGN OPTIONS

➤ This design would make a wonderful Christmas tree skirt. Draw Santa and his reindeer around the edge of a large circle.

➤ Try mirror-image Santas for a wider, bolder runner.

# THE BIRDS 1

**Finished Size: 15½" x 41"**

*Color photo on page 23*

This design features mama birds, baby birds, and trees filled with birds. It is a great year-round design that works in any color scheme.

This is a felt cutwork runner. Use felt and refer to the directions on page 10.

## MATERIALS

*Yardage is based on 60"-wide wool felt. Adjust the amounts if you change the size to fit your table.*

½ yd. white felt for background

½ yd. dark blue felt for top

18"-wide tracing paper

Size .01 Pigma pen

Dark blue machine-quilting thread

#16 sewing-machine needle

## CUTTING

Cut a 15½" x 41" piece each from the white felt, dark blue felt, and tracing paper.

## ASSEMBLY

*Use the patterns on pages 85–86.*

**1.** Using the Pigma pen, make a full-size drawing of your design elements on tracing paper. They can be arranged to fit the size and shape of the runner you want to make. Be sure to draw the borders, too (see facing page, bottom).

For this runner, I joined the 2 pattern sections, then traced the joined pattern 4 times (see facing page).

**2.** Layer the tracing paper with the background and top as shown in the diagram on page 10. Pin.

# TIP

Pattern 1, the bird, and its mirror image can be sewn in one continuous line. Pattern 2, in each corner, can also be sewn in one line. This means the entire table runner can be sewn in 6 continuous sections. Trace over each line with your finger before you begin, to get a feel for the direction the stitching will follow.

Trace patterns 1 and 2 onto 8½" x 11" pieces of tracing paper,
then join and tape patterns along dashed lines.

Flip joined pattern over. Trace over all lines from
the back to create a mirror-image pattern.

Mirror-image pattern

Regular pattern

Crease

Mirror-image pattern upside down

Regular pattern upside down

Fold your 15½" x 41" piece of tracing paper in half, then in half again. Open out.
Use your pattern and mirror-image pattern to fill in the 4 quadrants marked by the creases.

**3.** Thread the machine (top and bobbin) with the dark blue quilting thread and use the #16 needle. Stitch the straight outside borders first. This will keep the tracing paper in place for the next step. The paper may wrinkle and crease, but a little wrinkling is okay.

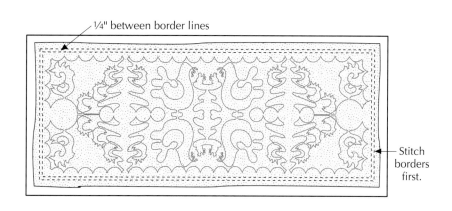

¼" between border lines

Stitch borders first.

**4.** Adjust your sewing machine for free motion-quilting (see page 10). Before you begin stitching, pull the bobbin thread up to the paper side. Stitch over all the traced lines. Tear away the tracing paper when the stitching is complete.

**5.** Cut away the top felt, following the directions on page 10. In the runner on page 23, I pinked the inside edges of the trees and flowers. All other edges are smooth. "Little Birds" (page 22) has no pinked edges, and the tree and flower centers are intact. Decide on the look you want and cut accordingly.

**6.** Sign and date your table runner.

## Design Options

➤ Try mirroring sections 1 and 2 in different ways:

# HAPPY BIRTHDAY, LITTLE BEAR!

**Finished Size: 14" x 41"**

*Color photo on page 25*

Who can resist the excitement of a child antici-
pating a birthday? Youngsters radiate the
wonder and pride of getting to hold up one more
finger when asked, "How old are you?" Here is a
runner to help set the stage, both before and during
the celebration. Let your children decide which
animal should be which color or what gifts the
animal friends should carry to the party. Add or
subtract candles to fit the child's age.

The runner in the photo on page 25 is all cotton,
so the following directions are for the "Cotton
Mini-Fuse" technique on page 9. You could also
make this runner out of wool or felt.

## MATERIALS

*Yardage is based on 44"-wide cotton fabric. Adjust the
yardage amounts if you change the size to fit your table.*

½ yd. gold solid for background

¼ yd. pink solid for borders, appliqué, and binding

6 assorted fat quarters for appliqué, tongues, and
binding

3" x 3" piece of off-white for candles and cartoon
bubble

½ yd. for backing

Embroidery floss to match the appliqué fabrics

Lightweight fusible web (omit for wool or felt)

Size .01 Pigma pens in assorted colors

## CUTTING

*Use the patterns on pages 87–95.*

From the gold fabric, cut a 14" x 35" piece for
the background.

From the pink fabric, cut 2 strips, each
3½" x 14", for the borders.

From the assorted fat quarters, the remaining
pink fabric, and the off-white fabric, cut out and
prepare the appliqué pieces, following the
directions for "Cotton Mini-Fuse" on page 9.
Remember to reverse the patterns in the book (see
page 8).

Using a Pigma pen, trace the lettering in the
cartoon bubble. Use the pattern provided, or draft
your own.

Cut 28 assorted 2¼" x 3¼" rectangles for the
tongues. Round off the corners, either freehand or
using the pattern provided on page 96. Do not
make any pink tongues.

From the remaining assorted fabrics and the
pink fabric, cut 1½"-wide strips of different lengths.
Be sure all the edges are straight and the corners
are square. Join the strips end to end until you have
a strip at least 120" long for binding (see page 13).

From the backing fabric, cut a piece 14" x 41".

## ASSEMBLY

**1.** Lay out all of the pieces before fusing anything to the background. Since most pieces overlap, the balloons are the only things that can be easily added later. When you are pleased with the arrangement, fuse. Be sure to follow the manufacturer's instructions.

**2.** Using the Pigma pens, draw in all of the details. Embroider over the details if desired.

**3.** Using matching embroidery floss, blanket stitch the pieces in place.

**4.** Add the embroidered details, following the patterns for placement.

**5.** Fuse, appliqué, and embroider the balloons and ribbons.

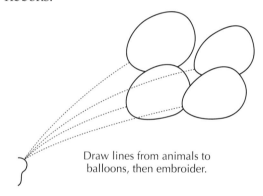

Draw lines from animals to balloons, then embroider.

**6.** To make cotton tongues, randomly pair up assorted tongue pieces. You should have a total of 14 pairs. Stitch, following the directions on page 15.

Arrange 7 tongues on each pink border strip as shown, with right sides together and raw edges even. Baste ¼" from the raw edge.

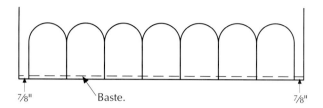

7⁄8"        Baste.                                    7⁄8"

**7.** Place a border strip on one end of the runner with right sides together, raw edges even, and the rounded ends of the tongues pointing toward the appliqué. Stitch. Press the seam allowances toward the runner. Repeat at the other end of the runner.

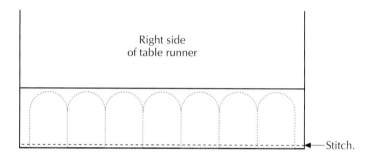

Right side
of table runner

Stitch.

**8.** Lay the runner on the backing with wrong sides together. Bind with the pieced binding (see pages 13–14), being careful not to catch the tongues in the seam.

**9.** Sign and date your table runner.

## DESIGN OPTIONS

➤    Enlarge the Birthday Bear and his or her cake to make a special runner for your child's room. Let your child add another candle to the cake each year. Cut the candles from felt so they are easy to add.

➤    If you want a really big party, enlarge the runner and add more animals! An easy way to do this is to reverse the templates and put the reversed animals on the other side of the table as shown.

➤    To lengthen the runner, add more tongue borders. See the directions for "Harvest Waltz II," beginning on page 45, for one layout idea.

# RESOURCES

### Wool

King's Road
548 South Los Angeles Street
Los Angeles, CA 90013
1-800-433-1546

### Felt

National Nonwovens
PO Box 150
Easthampton, MA 01027

### Hand-Dyed Cotton

Country House Cottons
PO Box 375
Fayette, IA 52142

### Embroidery Floss

The DMC Corporation
10 Port Kearny
South Kearny, NJ 07032-4688

# ABOUT THE AUTHOR

Janet Carija Brandt has always loved making things. She has applied her talents to fashion display, illustration, and buying, along with graphic design and architectural modeling. She has hooked rugs, crocheted, and knit; sewn wearables, quilts, and dolls; and embroidered. Her work has been featured in the Fairfield Fashion Show, the *Fiberarts Design Book V*, and numerous magazines. Twice she was named an Outstanding Traditional American Craftsman by *Early American Life* magazine. She is the author of *WOW! Wool-on-Wool Folk Art Quilts* and *Folk Art Animals*, both published by That Patchwork Place.

Janet says she is still happily afflicted with "make-thing-itis" and feels blessed with a loving husband, two wonderful children, a roof over her head, and plenty of food on the table (with a table runner, of course!). "It just doesn't get any better."

# PATTERNS

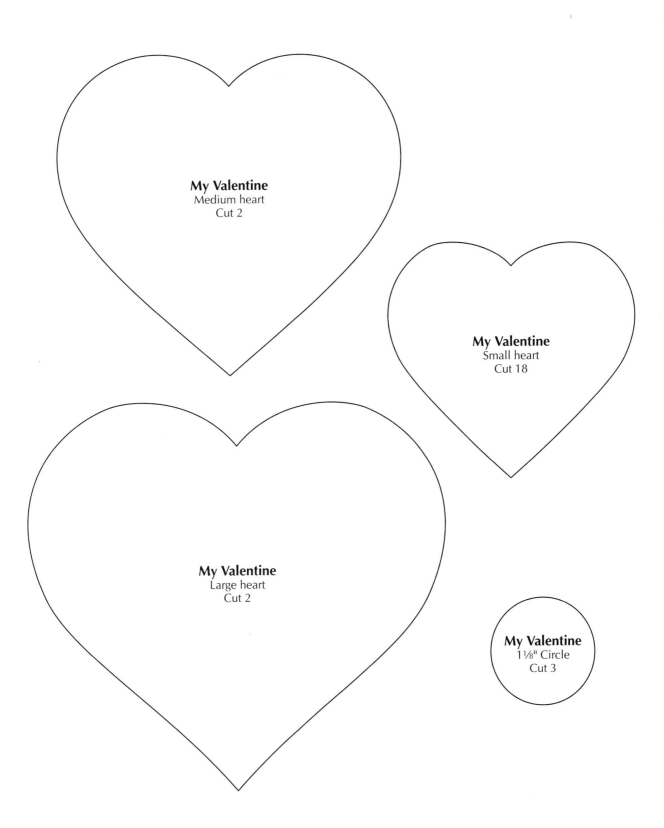

**My Valentine**
Medium heart
Cut 2

**My Valentine**
Small heart
Cut 18

**My Valentine**
Large heart
Cut 2

**My Valentine**
1⅛" Circle
Cut 3

**My Valentine**
Bird
Cut 2 and 2 reversed

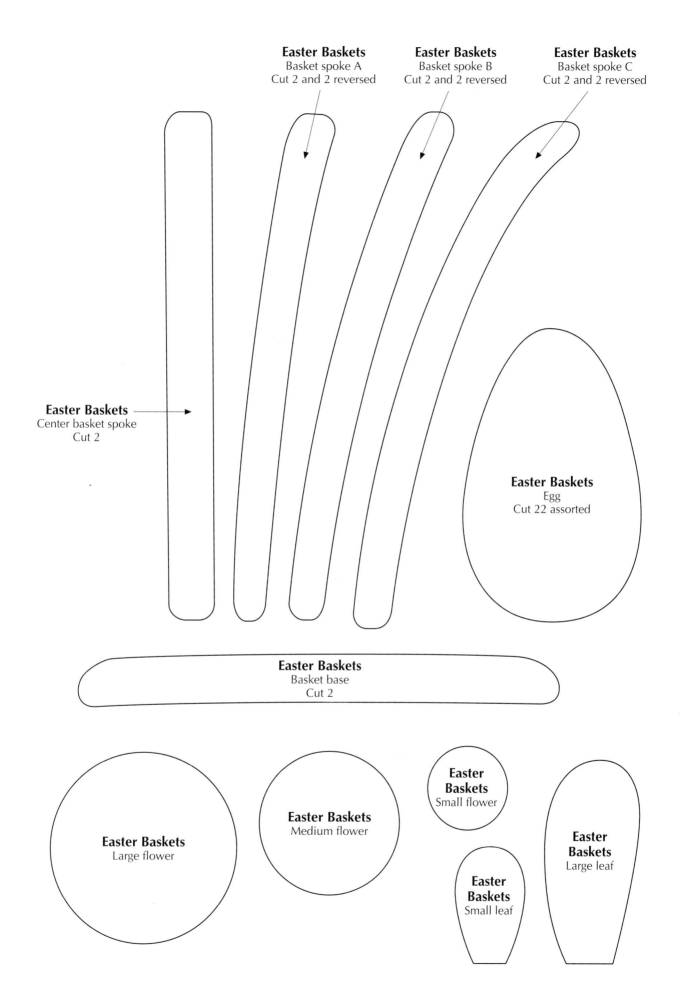

**Easter Baskets**
Basket spoke A
Cut 2 and 2 reversed

**Easter Baskets**
Basket spoke B
Cut 2 and 2 reversed

**Easter Baskets**
Basket spoke C
Cut 2 and 2 reversed

**Easter Baskets**
Center basket spoke
Cut 2

**Easter Baskets**
Egg
Cut 22 assorted

**Easter Baskets**
Basket base
Cut 2

**Easter Baskets**
Large flower

**Easter Baskets**
Medium flower

**Easter Baskets**
Small flower

**Easter Baskets**
Small leaf

**Easter Baskets**
Large leaf

**I'm a Little Teapot**
Teapot 1

Face

Apron

Flowers

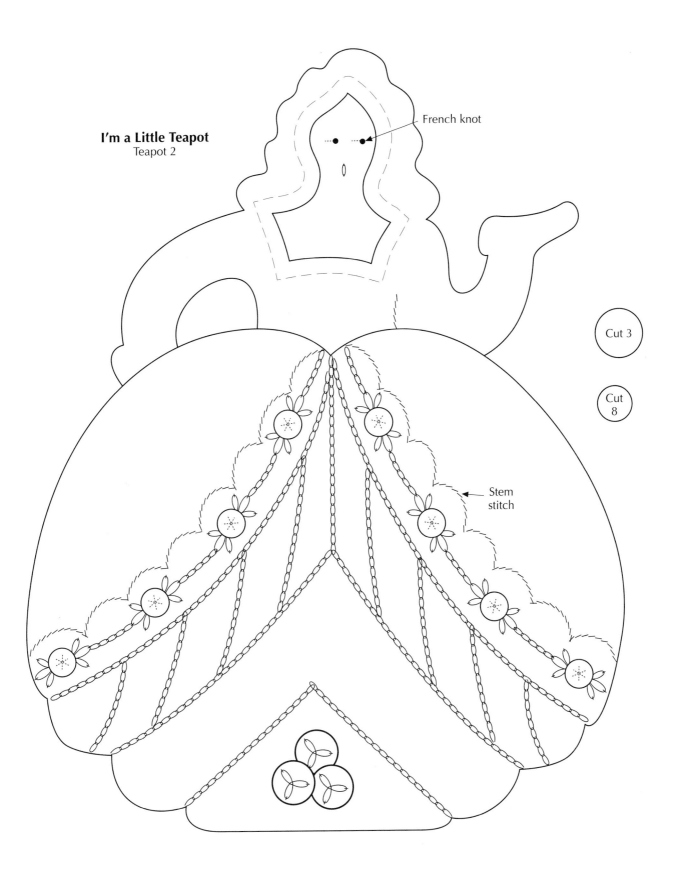

**I'm a Little Teapot**
Teapot 2

French knot

Cut 3

Cut 8

Stem stitch

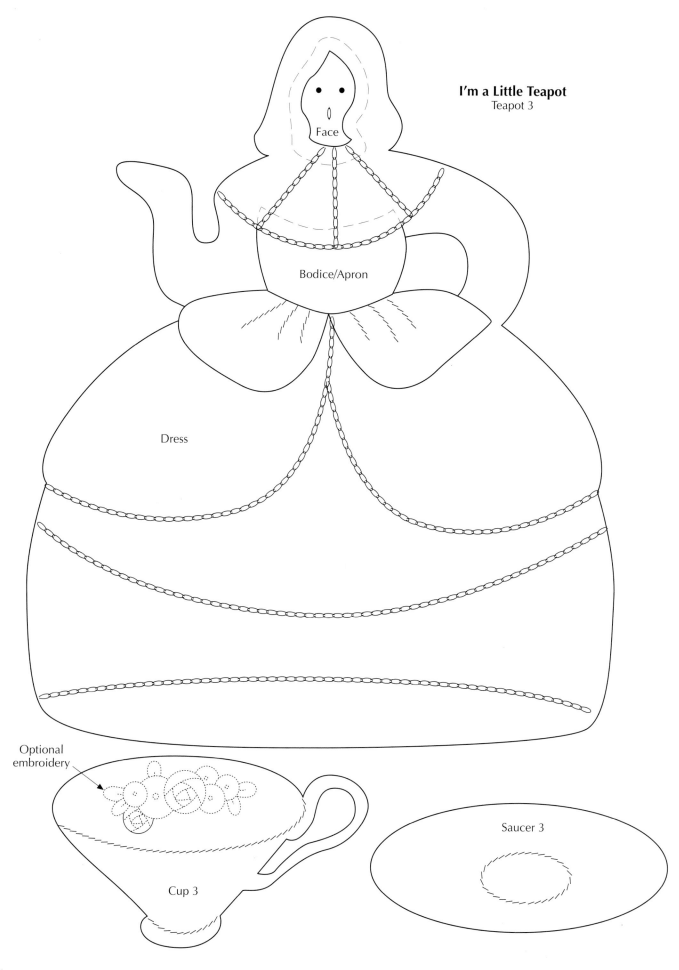

**I'm a Little Teapot**
Teapot 3

Face

Bodice/Apron

Dress

Optional embroidery

Cup 3

Saucer 3

## I'm a Little Teapot

Flower

Leaf

Teaspoon

Flower center

Cup 1

Saucer 1

Optional embroidery

Saucer 2

Cup 2

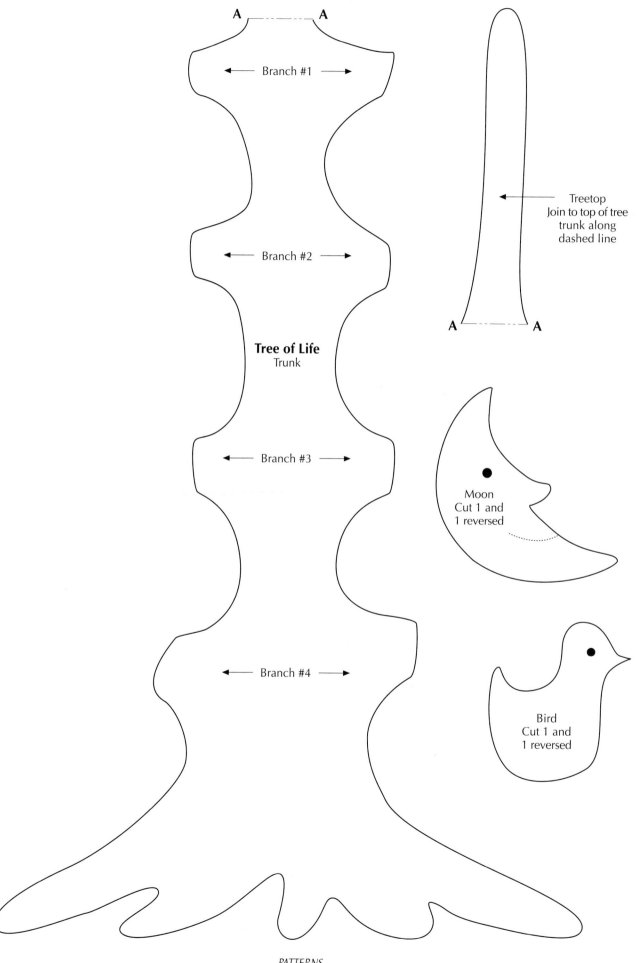

A        A

Branch #1

Branch #2

**Tree of Life**
Trunk

Branch #3

Branch #4

Treetop
Join to top of tree
trunk along
dashed line

A        A

Moon
Cut 1 and
1 reversed

Bird
Cut 1 and
1 reversed

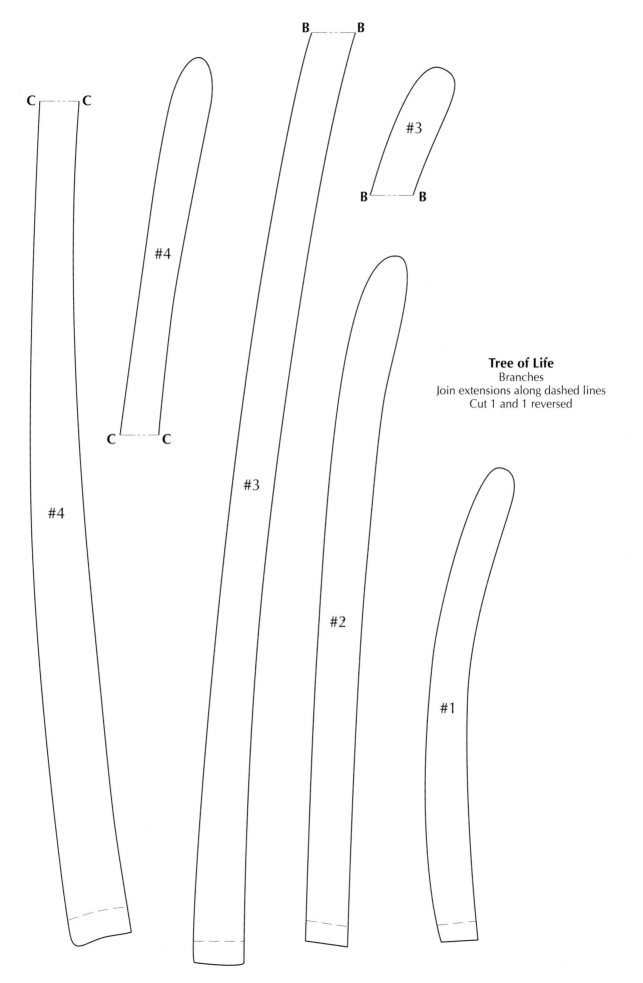

**Tree of Life**
Branches
Join extensions along dashed lines
Cut 1 and 1 reversed

**Tree of Life**

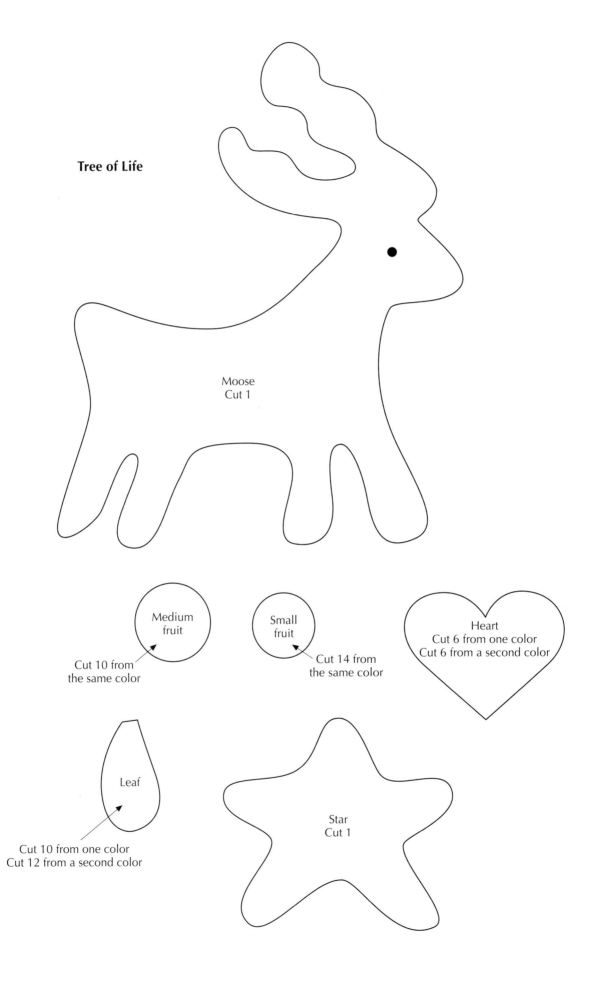

Moose
Cut 1

Medium
fruit

Cut 10 from
the same color

Small
fruit

Cut 14 from
the same color

Heart
Cut 6 from one color
Cut 6 from a second color

Leaf

Cut 10 from one color
Cut 12 from a second color

Star
Cut 1

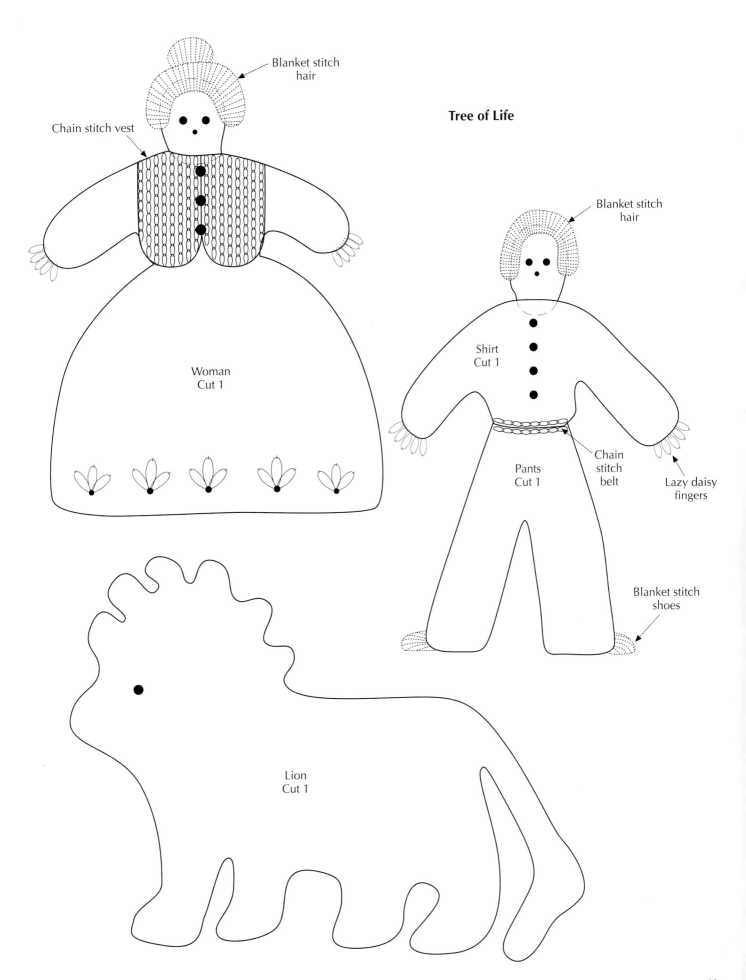

Blanket stitch hair

Chain stitch vest

**Tree of Life**

Blanket stitch hair

Shirt
Cut 1

Chain stitch belt

Lazy daisy fingers

Woman
Cut 1

Pants
Cut 1

Blanket stitch shoes

Lion
Cut 1

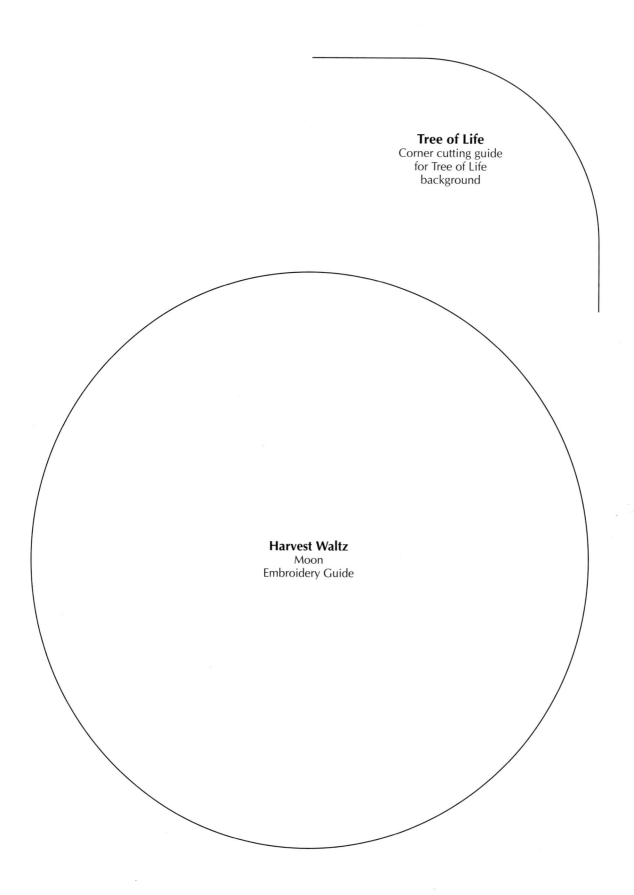

**Tree of Life**
Corner cutting guide
for Tree of Life
background

**Harvest Waltz**
Moon
Embroidery Guide

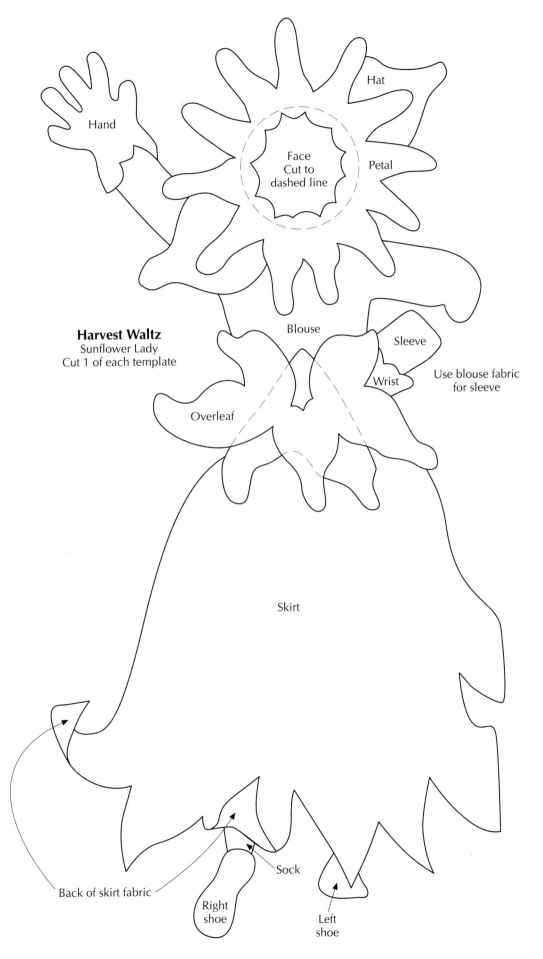

Hand

Hat

Face
Cut to
dashed line

Petal

**Harvest Waltz**
Sunflower Lady
Cut 1 of each template

Blouse

Sleeve

Wrist

Use blouse fabric
for sleeve

Overleaf

Skirt

Back of skirt fabric

Right
shoe

Sock

Left
shoe

**Harvest Waltz**
Scarecrow
Cut 1 of each template

Shirt

Left glove

Right glove

Coverall

Hat

Hair 2

Face

Hair 1

Collar

Boots

**Harvest Waltz**
Ms. Squash
Cut 1 of each template

Hat

Hat trim

Face

Collar

Blouse

Leaf

Left glove

Flower

Squash 1

Right glove

Squash 2

Squash 3

Skirt

Squash 4

Flowers/flower centers
Use contrasting colors

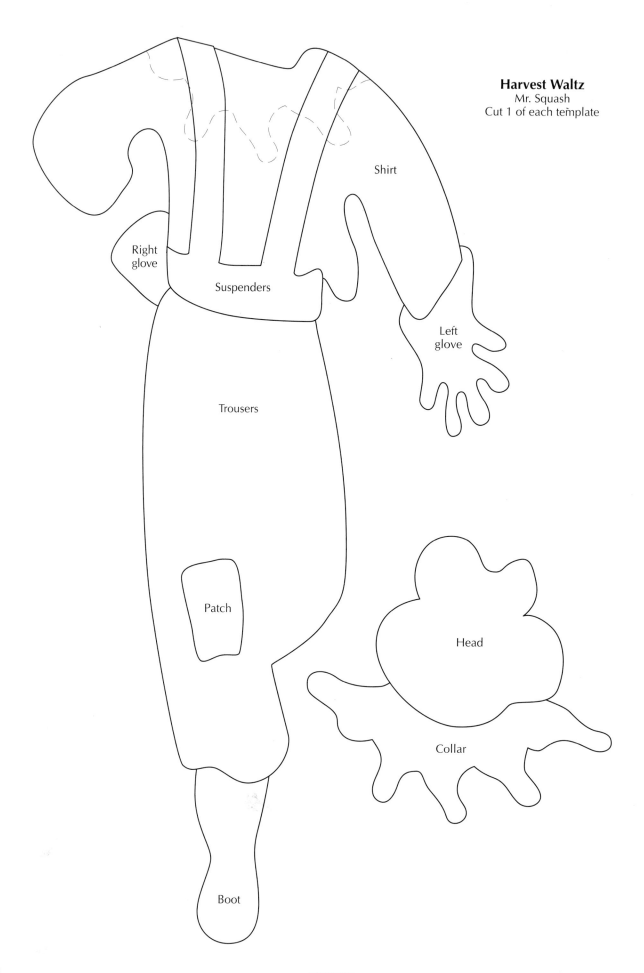

**Harvest Waltz**
Mr. Squash
Cut 1 of each template

Shirt

Right glove

Suspenders

Left glove

Trousers

Patch

Head

Collar

Boot

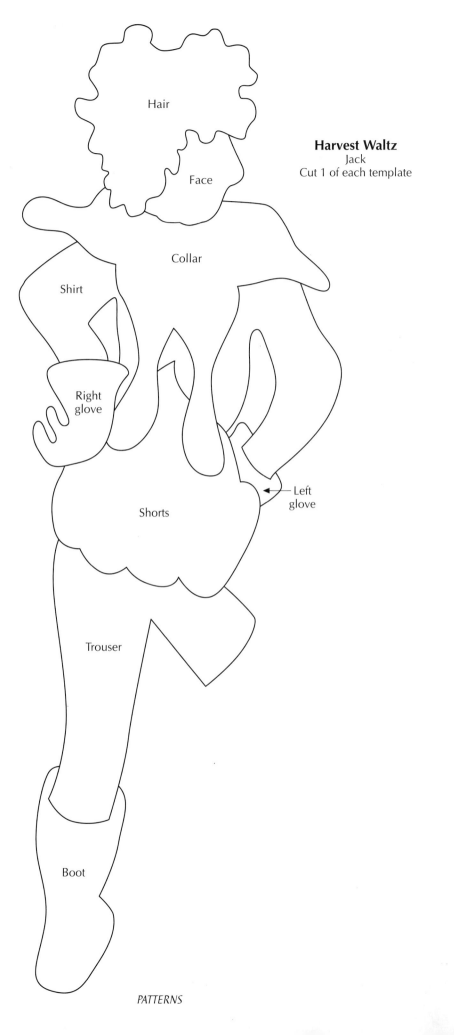

Hair

Face

**Harvest Waltz**
Jack
Cut 1 of each template

Collar

Shirt

Right
glove

Left
glove

Shorts

Trouser

Boot

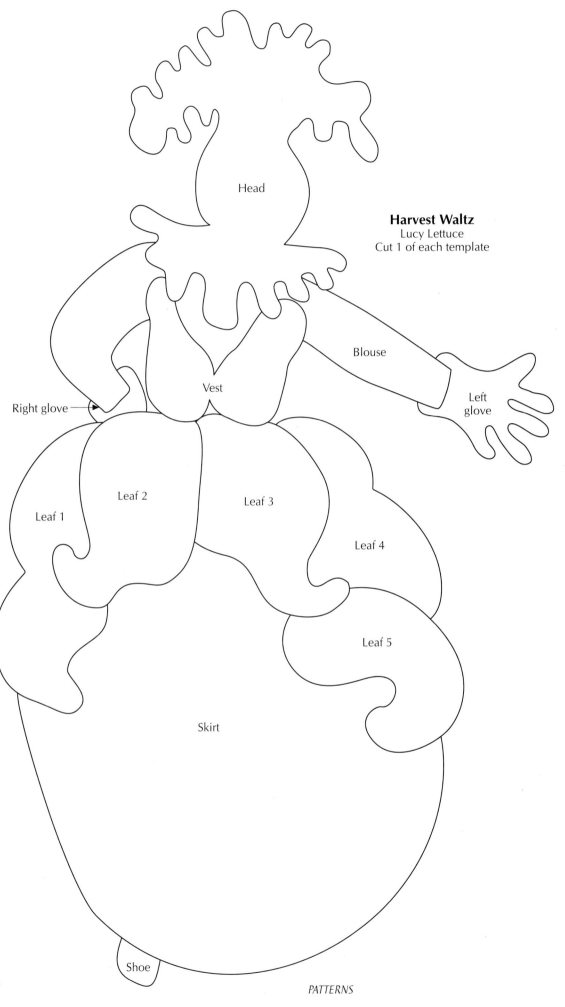

Head

**Harvest Waltz**
Lucy Lettuce
Cut 1 of each template

Blouse

Vest

Left glove

Right glove →

Leaf 2

Leaf 3

Leaf 1

Leaf 4

Leaf 5

Skirt

Shoe

French knots

**Harvest Waltz**
Sunflower Lady
Embroidery Guide

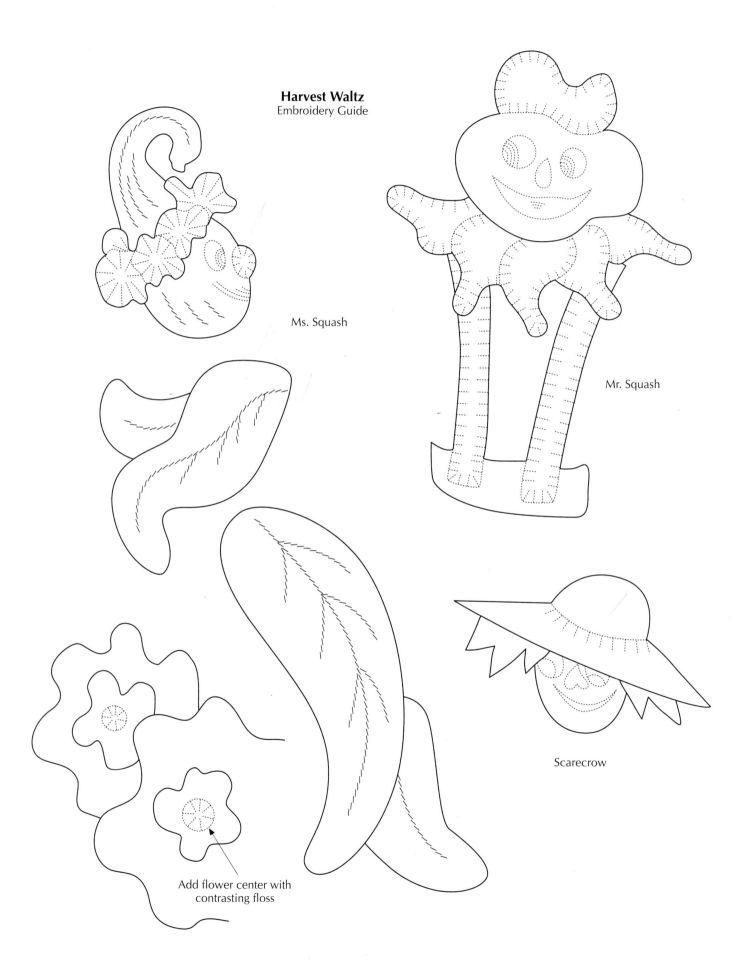

**Harvest Waltz**
Embroidery Guide

Ms. Squash

Mr. Squash

Scarecrow

Add flower center with
contrasting floss

*PATTERNS*

**Harvest Waltz**
Embroidery Guide

Jack

Lucy Lettuce

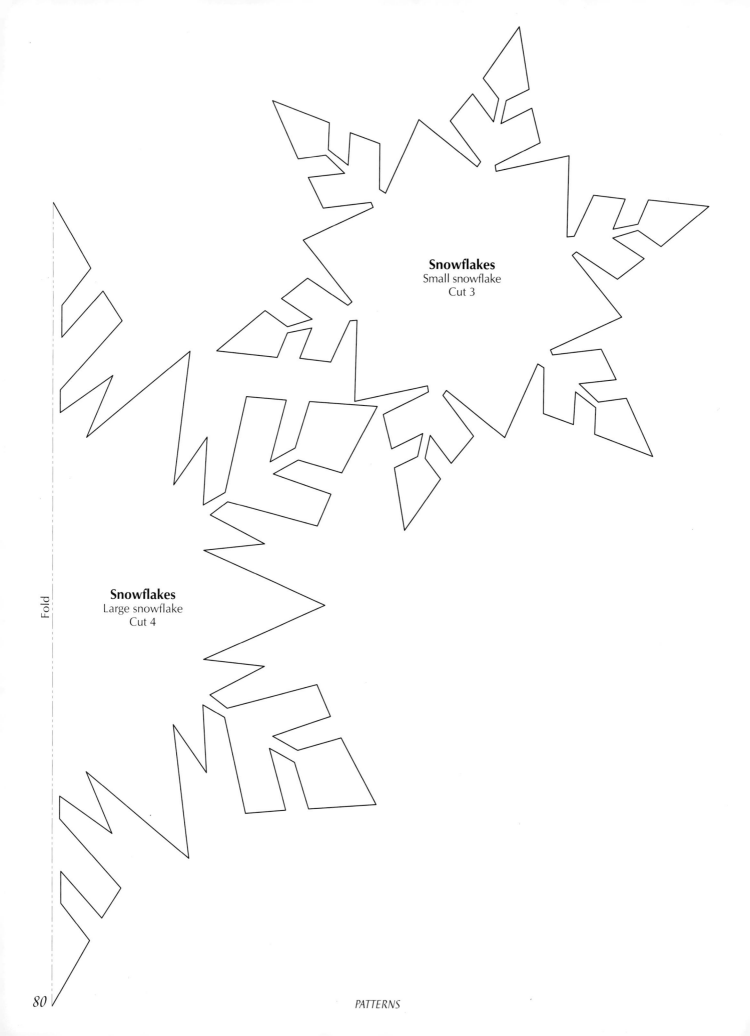

**Snowflakes**
Small snowflake
Cut 3

**Snowflakes**
Large snowflake
Cut 4

Fold

**Snowflakes**
Medium snowflake
Cut 3

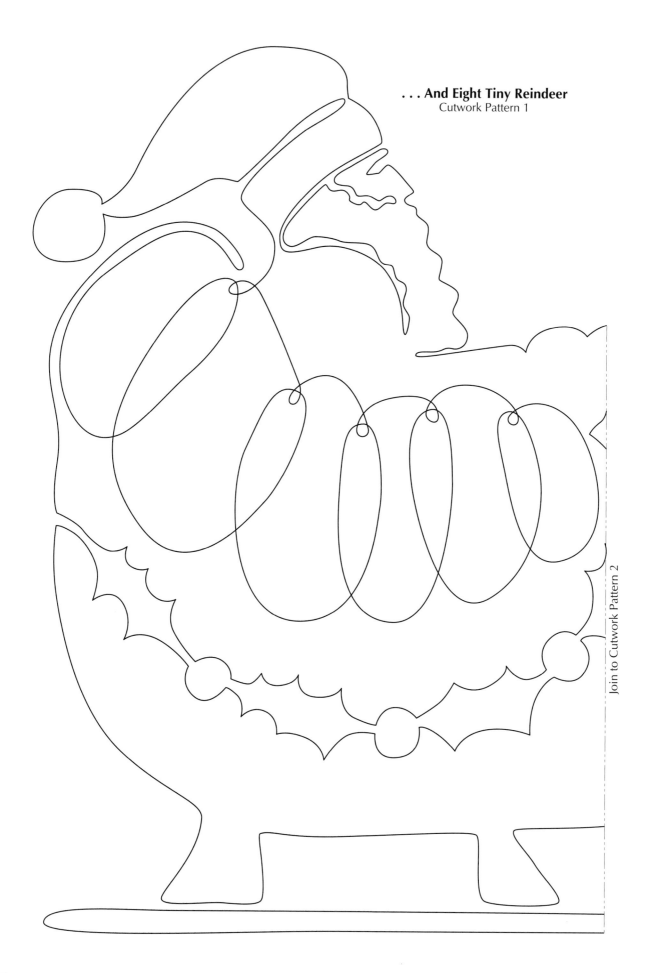

**. . . And Eight Tiny Reindeer**
Cutwork Pattern 1

Join to Cutwork Pattern 2

**. . . And Eight Tiny Reindeer**
Cutwork Pattern 2

Break line

Join to Cutwork Pattern 1

Join to Cutwork Pattern 3

Break line

Start
here

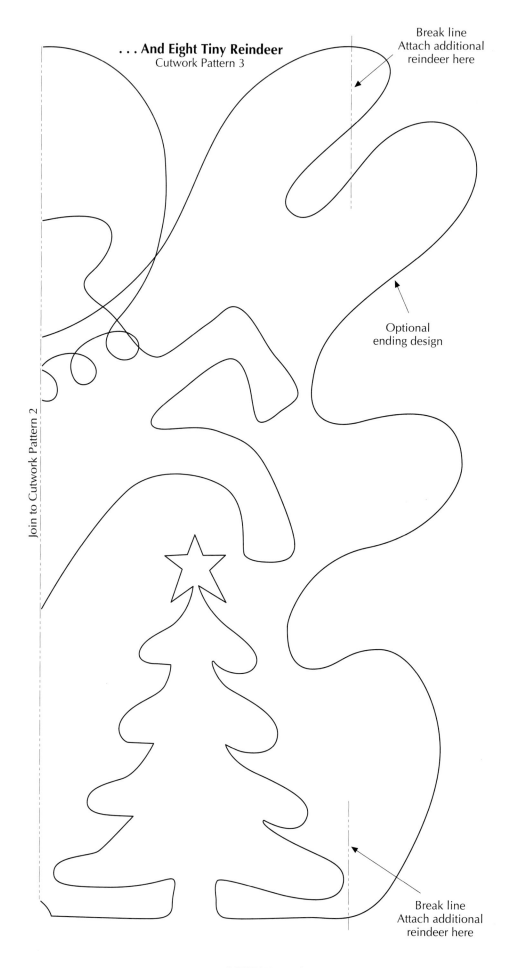

**. . . And Eight Tiny Reindeer**
Cutwork Pattern 3

Break line
Attach additional
reindeer here

Optional
ending design

Join to Cutwork Pattern 2

Break line
Attach additional
reindeer here

**The Birds**
Cutwork Pattern 1

**The Birds**
Cutwork Pattern 2

Join to Cutwork Pattern 1

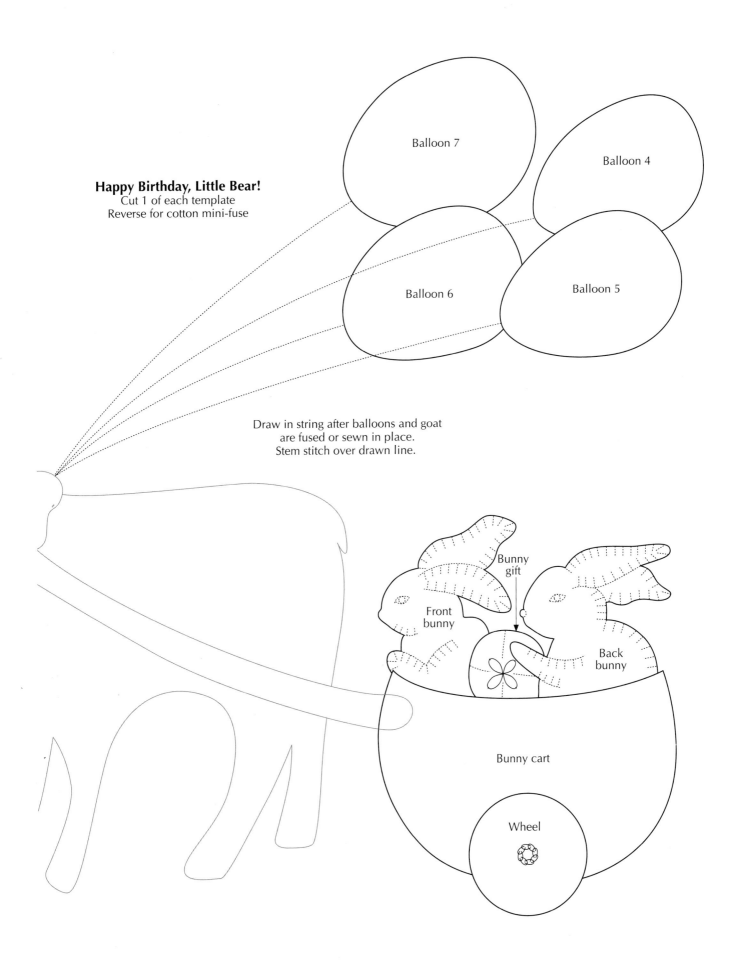

Balloon 7

Balloon 4

**Happy Birthday, Little Bear!**
Cut 1 of each template
Reverse for cotton mini-fuse

Balloon 6

Balloon 5

Draw in string after balloons and goat
are fused or sewn in place.
Stem stitch over drawn line.

Bunny
gift

Front
bunny

Back
bunny

Bunny cart

Wheel

# Happy Birthday, Little Bear!
Cut 1 of each template
Reverse for cotton mini-fuse

Bear hat

Bear

One piece

Sheep hat

Sheep nose

Embroider details

Sheep gift

Hooves

Sheep

Hooves

**Happy Birthday, Little Bear!**

Horns and body are all one piece. Use different-colored embroidery floss on horns.

Yoke

Ram

Hitch

Rooster

Legs

# Happy Birthday, Little Bear!
Cut 1 of each template
Reverse for cotton mini-fuse

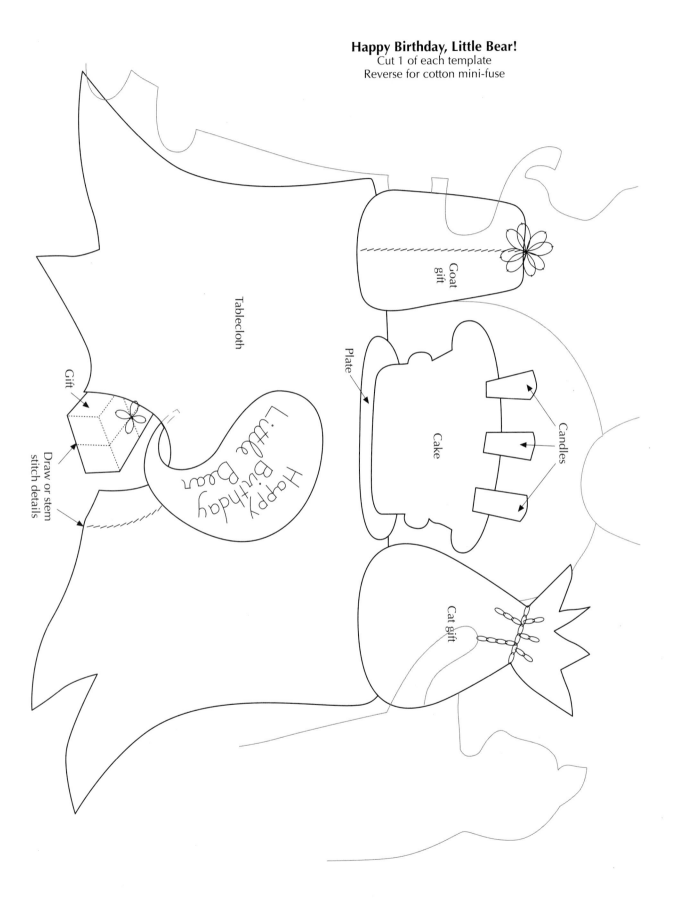

Tablecloth

Gift

Draw or stem
stitch details

Happy Birthday, Little Bear!

Goat gift

Plate

Cake

Candles

Cat gift

**Happy Birthday, Little Bear!**

Cat

**Happy Birthday, Little Bear!**
Cut 1 of each template
Reverse for cotton mini-fuse

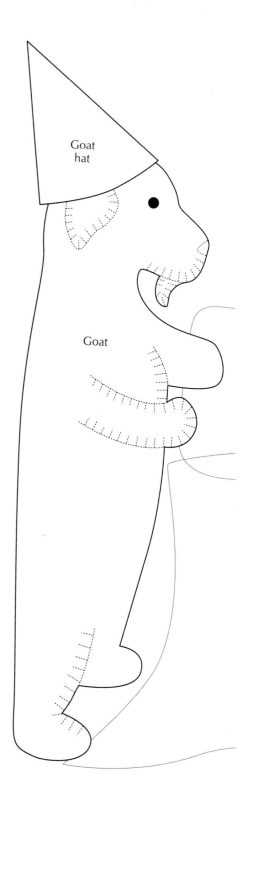

Goat
hat

Goat

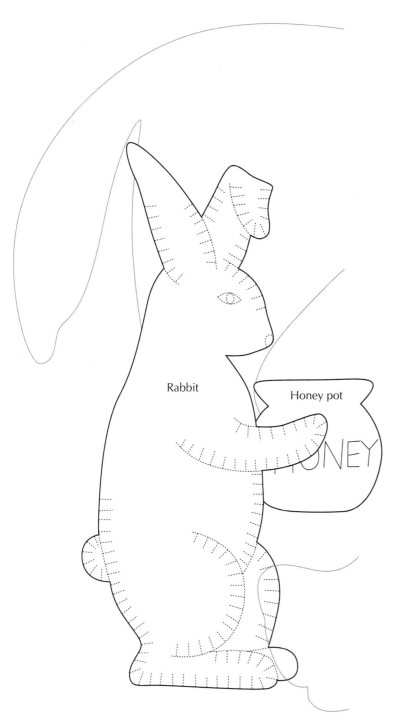

Rabbit

Honey pot

HONEY

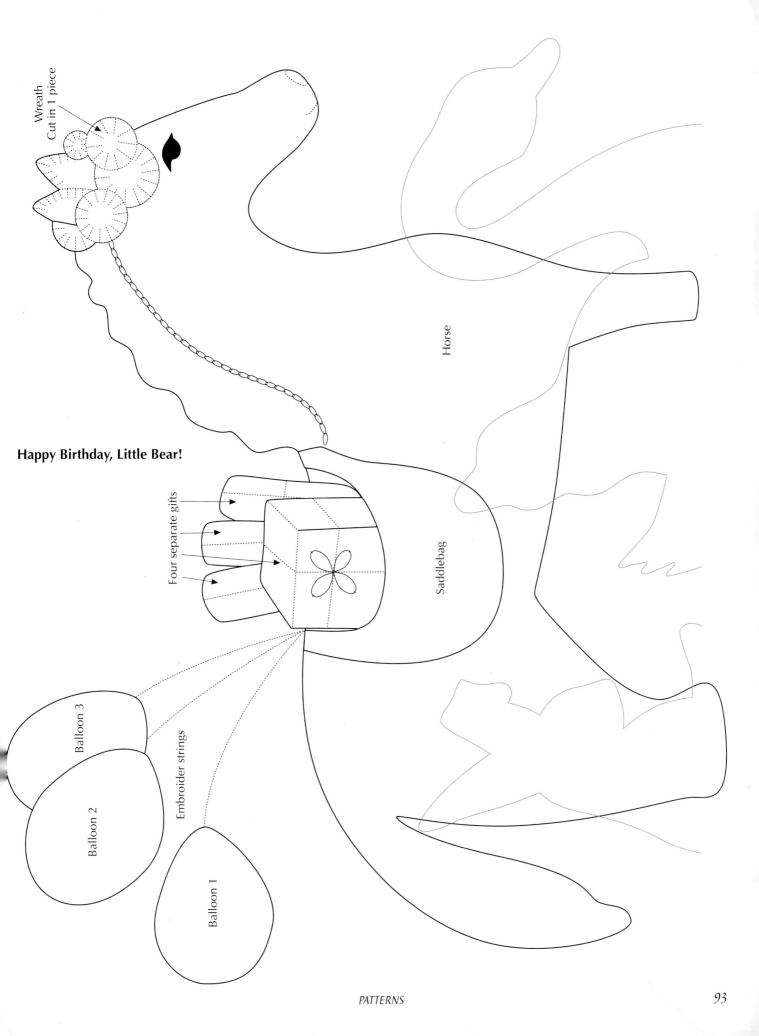

Wreath
Cut in 1 piece

Horse

**Happy Birthday, Little Bear!**

Four separate gifts

Saddlebag

Balloon 3

Balloon 2

Embroider strings

Balloon 1

## Happy Birthday, Little Bear!
Cut 1 of each template
Reverse for cotton mini-fuse

Cut baby ducks
as one piece

Embroider

Feet

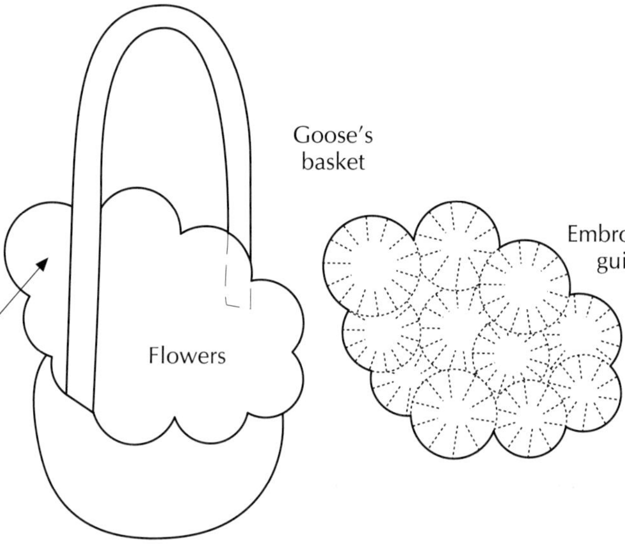

Goose's
basket

Flowers

Embroidery
guide

Cut out flowers as one piece
Embroider individual flowers

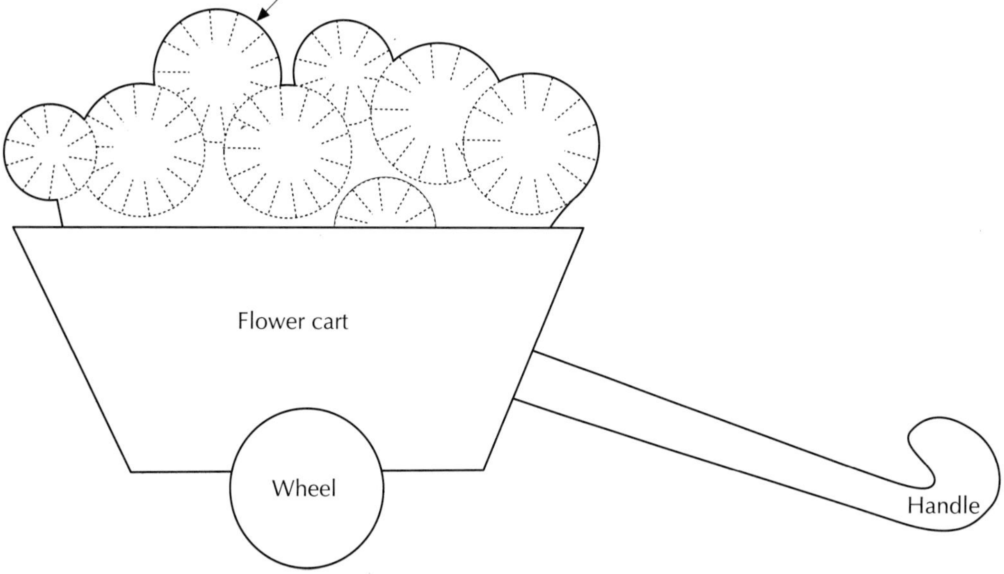

Flower cart

Wheel

Handle

# Happy Birthday, Little Bear!

Goose hat

Goose

Legs

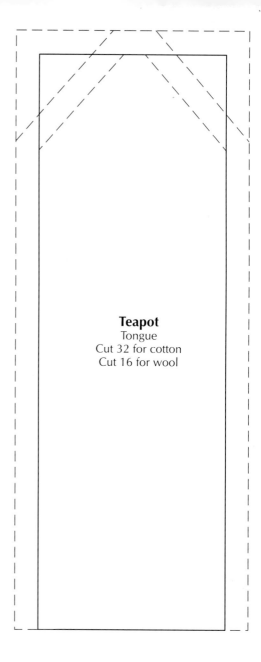

**Teapot**
Tongue
Cut 32 for cotton
Cut 16 for wool

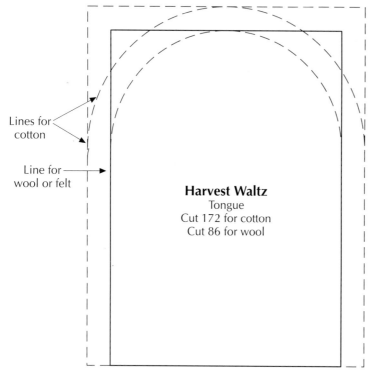

Lines for
cotton

Line for
wool or felt

**Harvest Waltz**
Tongue
Cut 172 for cotton
Cut 86 for wool

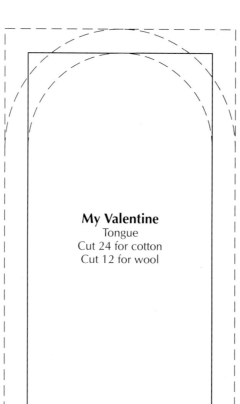

**My Valentine**
Tongue
Cut 24 for cotton
Cut 12 for wool

**Happy Birthday, Little Bear!**
Tongue
Cut 28 for cotton
Cut 14 for wool